D0102796

# Censorship

Noël Merino, *Book Editor*

**GREENHAVEN PRESS**
*A part of Gale, Cengage Learning*

GALE
CENGAGE Learning

Detroit • New York • San Francisco • New Haven, Conn • Waterville, Maine • London

Christine Nasso, *Publisher*
Elizabeth Des Chenes, *Managing Editor*

*For more information, contact:*
Greenhaven Press
27500 Drake Rd.
Farmington Hills, MI 48331-3535
Or you can visit our Internet site at gale.cengage.com

For product information and technology assistance, contact us at

Gale Customer Support, 1-800-877-4253
For permission to use material from this text or product, submit all requests online at www.cengage.com/permissions

Further permissions questions can be e-mailed to permissionrequest@cengage.com

Articles in Greenhaven Press anthologies are often edited for length to meet page requirements. In addition, original titles of these works are changed to clearly present the main thesis and to explicitly indicate the author's opinion. Every effort is made to ensure that Greenhaven Press accurately reflects the original intent of the authors. Every effort has been made to trace the owners of copyrighted material.

Cover image © Robert Maass/Documentary/Corbis

| LIBRARY OF CONGRESS CATALOGING-IN-PUBLICATION DATA |
| --- |
| Censorship / Noël Merino, book editor. |
| p. cm. -- (Introducing issues with opposing viewpoints) |
| Includes bibliographical references and index. |
| ISBN 978-0-7377-4731-7 (hardcover) |
| 1. Censorship--Juvenile literature. 2. Censorship--United States--Juvenile literature. 3. Freedom of speech--Juvenile literature. 4. Internet--Censorship--Juvenile literature. |
| I. Merino, Noël. |
| Z657.C394 2010 |
| 363.31--dc22 |
| 2009049142 |

Printed in the United States of America
1 2 3 4 5 6 7 14 13 12 11 10

# Contents

Foreword 5

Introduction 7

## Chapter 1: Should Free Speech Be Limited?

1. Free Speech Should Have Several Limits 12
   *Jonah Goldberg*

2. Free Speech Should Have Few Limits 17
   *American Civil Liberties Union*

3. Flag Destruction Is Speech That Should Be Protected 25
   *Cathy Young*

4. Flag Destruction Is Not Speech That Should Be Protected 31
   *Citizens Flag Alliance*

5. Hate Speech Sometimes Warrants Censorship 38
   *Faisal Kutty*

6. Self-Censorship of Offensive Speech Is Cowardly
   and Dangerous 44
   *Doug Marlette*

## Chapter 2: Can Censorship Be Justified as Protection for Children?

1. Decency Standards on Television Are Necessary to
   Protect Children 53
   *Parents Television Council*

2. Parents, Not Decency Standards, Should Regulate Television 60
   *Economist*

3. Parents Should Have a Say About Which Books End up
   in Schools 66
   *Warren Throckmorton*

4. Banning Books in Schools Promotes Ignorance and Intolerance 71
   *Thomas G. Palaima*

5. Students Need Freedom of Speech 76
   *Sara-Ellen Amster*

6. Students Can Rightfully Have Their Speech Limited 82
   *Janesville (WI) Gazette*

## Chapter 3: Do New Technologies Need Regulation?

1. Some Regulation Is Necessary for New Electronic Media 88
   *David Coursey*

2. Education on Use of New Electronic Media Is Better
   than Regulation 93
   *Paul K. McMasters*

3. Obscenity Laws Warrant Censorship of Internet Pornography 99
   *Robert Peters*

4. Obscenity Laws Should Be Eliminated 105
   *Marjorie Heins*

5. Library Internet Filters Are Necessary 112
   *Arlene Sawicki*

6. Library Internet Filters Threaten Freedom 118
   *Marjorie Heins, Christina Cho, and Ariel Feldman*

Facts About Censorship 123
Organizations to Contact 125
For Further Reading 130
Index 135
Picture Credits 140

# Foreword

Indulging in a wide spectrum of ideas, beliefs, and perspectives is a critical cornerstone of democracy. After all, it is often debates over differences of opinion, such as whether to legalize abortion, how to treat prisoners, or when to enact the death penalty, that shape our society and drive it forward. Such diversity of thought is frequently regarded as the hallmark of a healthy and civilized culture. As the Reverend Clifford Schutjer of the First Congregational Church in Mansfield, Ohio, declared in a 2001 sermon, "Surrounding oneself with only like-minded people, restricting what we listen to or read only to what we find agreeable is irresponsible. Refusing to entertain doubts once we make up our minds is a subtle but deadly form of arrogance." With this advice in mind, Introducing Issues with Opposing Viewpoints books aim to open readers' minds to the critically divergent views that comprise our world's most important debates.

Introducing Issues with Opposing Viewpoints simplifies for students the enormous and often overwhelming mass of material now available via print and electronic media. Collected in every volume is an array of opinions that captures the essence of a particular controversy or topic. Introducing Issues with Opposing Viewpoints books embody the spirit of nineteenth-century journalist Charles A. Dana's axiom: "Fight for your opinions, but do not believe that they contain the whole truth, or the only truth." Absorbing such contrasting opinions teaches students to analyze the strength of an argument and compare it to its opposition. From this process readers can inform and strengthen their own opinions, or be exposed to new information that will change their minds. Introducing Issues with Opposing Viewpoints is a mosaic of different voices. The authors are statesmen, pundits, academics, journalists, corporations, and ordinary people who have felt compelled to share their experiences and ideas in a public forum. Their words have been collected from newspapers, journals, books, speeches, interviews, and the Internet, the fastest growing body of opinionated material in the world.

Introducing Issues with Opposing Viewpoints shares many of the well-known features of its critically acclaimed parent series, Opposing Viewpoints. The articles are presented in a pro/con format, allowing readers to absorb divergent perspectives side by side. Active reading questions preface each viewpoint, requiring the student to approach the material thoughtfully and carefully. Useful charts, graphs, and cartoons supplement each article. A thorough introduction provides readers with crucial background on an issue. An annotated bibliography points the reader toward articles, books, and Web sites that contain additional information on the topic. An appendix of organizations to contact contains a wide variety of charities, nonprofit organizations, political groups, and private enterprises that each hold a position on the issue at hand. Finally, a comprehensive index allows readers to locate content quickly and efficiently.

Introducing Issues with Opposing Viewpoints is also significantly different from Opposing Viewpoints. As the series title implies, its presentation will help introduce students to the concept of opposing viewpoints and learn to use this material to aid in critical writing and debate. The series' four-color, accessible format makes the books attractive and inviting to readers of all levels. In addition, each viewpoint has been carefully edited to maximize a reader's understanding of the content. Short but thorough viewpoints capture the essence of an argument. A substantial, thought-provoking essay question placed at the end of each viewpoint asks the student to further investigate the issues raised in the viewpoint, compare and contrast two authors' arguments, or consider how one might go about forming an opinion on the topic at hand. Each viewpoint contains sidebars that include at-a-glance information and handy statistics. A Facts About section located in the back of the book further supplies students with relevant facts and figures.

Following in the tradition of the Opposing Viewpoints series, Greenhaven Press continues to provide readers with invaluable exposure to the controversial issues that shape our world. As John Stuart Mill once wrote: "The only way in which a human being can make some approach to knowing the whole of a subject is by hearing what can be said about it by persons of every variety of opinion and studying all modes in which it can be looked at by every character of mind. No wise man ever acquired his wisdom in any mode but this." It is to this principle that Introducing Issues with Opposing Viewpoints books are dedicated.

# Introduction

*"As a matter of constitutional tradition, in the absence of evidence to the contrary, we presume that governmental regulation of the content of speech is more likely to interfere with the free exchange of ideas than to encourage it. The interest in encouraging freedom of expression in a democratic society outweighs any theoretical but unproven benefit of censorship."*

—John Paul Stevens, *Reno v. American Civil Liberties Union* (1997)

Censorship is the act of suppressing communicative material (in print, in images, in art) because it is considered too dangerous or objectionable to be consumed. One area in which censorship has a long history throughout the world is pornography, the depiction of sexual subject matter for the purpose of eliciting sexual desire. In 1969, however, the U.S. Supreme Court ruled in *Stanley v. Georgia* that the private possession of pornography in one's home is constitutionally protected by the First Amendment. At the time, this decision protected pornographic material in film, literature, photographs, and art, but the case was heard well before the advent of the Internet and all the pornography contained within. This new venue for the distribution of pornography has created a fierce debate about in what ways, if any, pornography on the Internet can and should be regulated or censored.

Many different kinds of pornography, whether in print, picture, or film, have gone through periods of complete censorship in different parts of the world. In Iran, Malaysia, and Vietnam, for example, all pornography is currently illegal. In the United States, two kinds of pornography are prohibited: child pornography and material deemed "obscene" by the test developed in the 1973 Supreme Court case *Miller v. California*. This three-pronged test is notoriously subjective. It requires: 1) that the average person finds the work to appeal to prurient interest (causing sexual desire); 2) that the work is patently offensive, and 3) that the work lacks artistic, political, or scientific

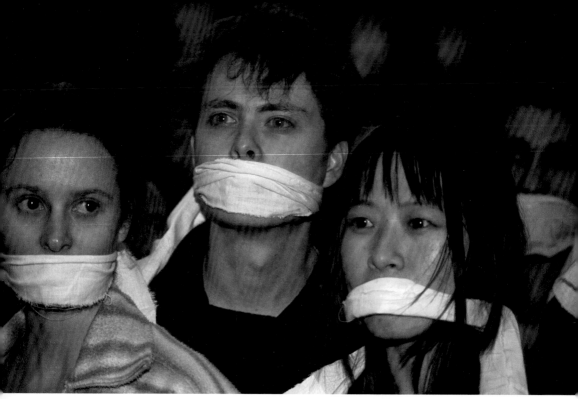

*What subjects and speech should and should not be censored has been a point of controversy since the formation of the American republic.*

value. It is not always clear exactly what material meets the three conditions of the *Miller* test, and one notable problem is that it relies on community standards, thus making it possible that certain pornography may be legal in Los Angeles but not in Memphis, or vice versa. Courts are frequently asked to make decisions on this issue, although pornography in a variety of forms currently remains widely available.

The issue of children is central to the pornography debate. Child pornography—that is, pornography depicting anyone under the age of eighteen—is illegal in the United States. In addition, even legal pornography must be adequately shielded from children under the age of eighteen. Thus, according to the law, pornography must be censored unless the consumers are adults. For this reason, pornographic magazines are sold behind counters, often covered in plain wrappers to prevent any minors seeing the covers. Similarly, pornographic videos can be rented only to adults aged eighteen and over. The Internet, however, currently has no reliable method for screening people's ages, and pornographic Web sites generally rely on the viewer to report his or her age, without verification, making it easy for minors to have access to free pornography on the Internet.

Several attempts have been made by Congress to pass legislation to protect children who use the Internet. The first of these attempts is the Communications Decency Act of 1996 (CDA). Under CDA, individuals would be subject to criminal sanctions for using a computer to send "obscene or indecent" messages to a minor or displaying material that could be seen by a minor that "depicts or describes, in terms patently offensive as measured by contemporary community standards, sexual or excretory activities or organs."[1] The Supreme Court, however, in *Reno v. American Civil Liberties Union* (1997), found the indecency provisions of CDA unconstitutional under the First Amendment, which protects freedom of speech.

After the failure of the CDA, Congress passed the Child Online Protection Act (COPA) of 1998. COPA targeted commercial distributors with the responsibility of protecting access to their sites containing "any material that is harmful to minors"[2] and defined as obscenity under the *Miller* test. The law states that any sexual content and lewd nudity designed to pander to prurient interest, lacking value for minors, qualified. COPA imposed civil and criminal penalties on violators, but it was quickly challenged in the courts on charges of violating the First Amendment. The courts agreed, and COPA was finally eliminated in January 2009, when the Supreme Court refused to review a lower federal court decision finding the law to unconstitutionally limit the free speech of adults, thus violating the First Amendment.

Finally, the Children's Internet Protection Act (CIPA) of 2000 was passed to protect children from Internet pornography at public libraries. CIPA requires public libraries that receive federal subsidies for computing to use filtering software to prevent children from seeing pornography on the library computers. CIPA does, however, require that the software be disabled upon request by an adult patron. The American Civil Liberties Union challenged CIPA, but in 2003 the Supreme Court in *United States v. American Library Association* ruled that CIPA did not violate the First Amendment. Several libraries around the country have chosen to do without federal funds rather than install the filtering software required by CIPA.

The issue of censorship of pornography is one with a long, contentious past. To this day, many Americans call for complete censorship of pornography. However, the First Amendment protection for adult viewing of pornography in private is strong in the United States. For the formats, like magazines, that are easily restricted from minors, the application of an age requirement has been relatively straightforward. With the advent and growth of the Internet, however, the issue of protecting children becomes more complicated. Many have called for highly restricted access, if not outright censorship, of pornography on the Internet. This topic is one of the many ongoing debates about censorship. The issues of whether speech can ever be rightfully limited, the extent to which protecting children justifies censorship, and the challenge of new technologies are explored in *Introducing Issues with Opposing Viewpoints: Censorship.*

## Notes
1. Federal Communications Commission, Communications Decency Act of 1996, www.fcc.gov/Reports/tcom1996.txt.
2. Child Online Protection Act, H.R. 3783.

# Chapter 1

# Should Free Speech Be Limited?

The Ku Klux Klan consistently advocates racial supremacy and uses hate speech at their rallies. Many advocate limits on the right to use hate speech.

**Viewpoint**

**1**

# Free Speech Should Have Several Limits

*"The First Amendment was not intended to protect pornographers, strippers or the subsidies of avant-garde artistes."*

## Jonah Goldberg

In the following viewpoint Jonah Goldberg argues that free speech protected by the First Amendment was never meant to protect the sort of speech that it has been interpreted to protect. Goldberg contends that the right to free expression is clearly not absolute, giving evidence of several exceptions to freedom of speech that he believes are justified. Until two recent U.S. Supreme Court decisions, Goldberg claims, unimportant speech has been protected and important speech has been constrained. Goldberg is a syndicated columnist and editor at large at *National Review Online.* He is the author of *Liberal Fascism: The Secret History of the American Left from Mussolini to the Politics of Meaning.*

AS YOU READ, CONSIDER THE FOLLOWING QUESTIONS:
1. According to Goldberg, what was the reason that free-speech rights were protected in the U.S. Constitution?
2. What did the U.S. Supreme Court deregulate in the 1960s and 1970s, according to the author, as a part of safeguarding free speech?
3. Goldberg argues that unimportant speech has been protected while what kind of speech has been under attack?

Jonah Goldberg, "Supreme Speech," *National Review Online,* June 29, 2007. Copyright © 2007 Tribune Media Services, Inc. Reprinted with permission.

T here are few areas where I think common sense is more sorely lacking than in our public debates over free speech, and there's no better proof than two recent Supreme Court decisions.

## Commonsense Limits on Speech

But before we go there, let me state plainly where I'm coming from. First and foremost: The more overtly political the speech is, the more protected it must be. The First Amendment was not intended to protect pornographers, strippers or the subsidies of avant-garde artistes who think the state should help defray the costs of homoerotica and sacrilegious art. This isn't to say that "artistic" expression doesn't deserve some protection, but come on. Our free-speech rights were enshrined in the Constitution to guarantee private citizens—rich and poor alike—the right to criticize government without fear of retribution.

Now, there are commonsense exceptions to this principle. Not only can the state ban screaming "fire!" in a crowded movie theater, it can ban screaming "Vote for Cheney in '08!" in a theater, too (or, more properly, it can help theater owners enforce their bans on such behavior).

A better example of an exception would be schools. Students can't say whatever they want in

school, whenever they want to say it, because schools are special institutions designed to create citizens out of the malleable clay of youth. Children aren't grown-ups, which is one of the reasons why we call them "children."

Making citizens requires a little benign tyranny, as any teacher (or parent) will tell you. If this weren't obvious, after-school detention would be treated like imprisonment and homework like involuntary servitude.

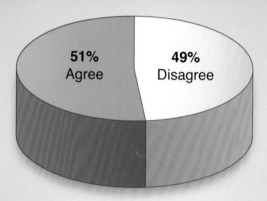

**Freedom of speech should not extend to groups that sympathize with terrorists:**

51%
Agree

49%
Disagree

Taken from: Pew Research Center, "Trends in Political Values and Core Attitudes: 1987–2009," May 21, 2009. www.pewresearch.org.

## The Outer Boundaries of Acceptable Speech

For a long time, we concluded the best way to protect political speech was to defend other forms of expression—commercial, artistic, and just plain wacky—so as to make sure that our core right to political speech was kept safe. Like establishing outposts in hostile territory, we safeguarded the outer boundaries of acceptable expression to keep the more important home fire of political speech burning freely. That's why in the 1960s and 1970s, all sorts of stuff—pornography, strip clubs, etc.—was deregulated by the Supreme Court on the grounds that this was now legitimate "expression" of some sort.

Also, in 1969, the Supreme Court ruled in *Tinker v. Des Moines*, that students don't "shed their constitutional rights to freedom of speech or expression at the schoolhouse gate."

This always struck me as preposterous. Of course students shed some of their rights at the schoolhouse gate. That's the whole idea behind the concept of *in loco parentis* [in the place of a parent]. Teachers and administrators get to act like your parents while you're at school. And parents are not required to respect the constitutional rights of their kids. Tell me, do hall-pass requirements restrict the First Amendment right of free assembly? Don't many of the same people who claim that you have free-speech rights in public schools also insist that you don't have the right to pray in them?

## The Important Speech to Protect
Still, such buffoonery would be pardonable if the grand bargain of defending marginal speech so as to better fortify the protective cocoon around sacrosanct political speech were still in effect. But that bargain fell apart almost from the get-go. At the same moment we were letting our freak flags fly when it came to unimportant speech, we started turning the screws on political speech. After Watergate, campaign-finance laws started restricting what independent political groups could say and when they could say it, culminating in the McCain-Feingold law [Bipartisan Campaign Reform Act of 2002] that barred "outside" criticism of politicians when it would matter most—i.e., around an election.

And that's why we live in a world where cutting NEA [National Endowment for the Arts] grants is called censorship, a student's "Bong

*Despite the fact that the U.S. Supreme Court ruled in* Tinker v. Des Moines *that students have free speech rights in school, they still have to obey the rules laid out by school administrators.*

Hits 4 Jesus" sign is hailed as vital political speech, and a group of citizens asking fellow citizens to petition their elected representatives to change their minds is supposedly guilty of illegal speech.

That is until this week [June 25–29, 2007]. In one case [*Morse v. Frederick*], the Supreme Court ruled that a student attending a mandatory school event can be disciplined by the school's principal for holding up a sign saying "Bong Hits 4 Jesus," and in another [*Federal Election Commission v. Wisconsin Right to Life, Inc.*] it ruled that a pro-life group can, in fact, urge citizens to contact their senators even if one of the senators happens to be running for re-election. Staggeringly, these were close and controversial calls.

Many self-described liberals and reformers think it should be the other way around. Teenage students should have unfettered free-speech rights, while grown-up citizens should stay quiet, like good little boys and girls. Thank goodness at least five Supreme Court justices disagreed.

**EVALUATING THE AUTHOR'S ARGUMENTS:**

In this viewpoint Goldberg argues that one example of speech that is not protected by the First Amendment is student speech in schools. Give one example of a kind of speech (either verbal or symbolic) that students are not allowed to express in school.

# Free Speech Should Have Few Limits

> *"If we do not come to the defense of the free speech rights of the most unpopular among us . . . then no one's liberty will be secure."*

### American Civil Liberties Union

In the following viewpoint the American Civil Liberties Union (ACLU) contends that the First Amendment right to freedom of expression is central to the exercise of other fundamental rights. Accordingly, the ACLU believes that freedom of expression, including freedom of speech, needs strong protection. The ACLU argues that even unpopular expression, such as hate speech and expression that some find obscene, should be protected. The ACLU is an organization that works in courts, legislatures, and communities to protect the individual rights guaranteed by the Constitution and laws of the United States.

**AS YOU READ, CONSIDER THE FOLLOWING QUESTIONS:**

1. In what year, according to the American Civil Liberties Union (ACLU), did the Supreme Court first hear a case regarding free speech issues?
2. According to the ACLU, the First Amendment protects what kind of speech besides the "pure speech" in books, newspapers, leaflets, and rallies?
3. What kind of historically unprotected expression does the ACLU worry invites government abuse?

Freedom of speech, of the press, of association, of assembly and petition—this set of guarantees, protected by the First Amendment, comprises what we refer to as freedom of expression. The Supreme Court has written that this freedom is "the matrix, the indispensable condition of nearly every other form of freedom." Without it, other fundamental rights, like the right to vote, would wither and die.

## Free Speech Needs Protection

But in spite of its "preferred position" in our constitutional hierarchy, the nation's commitment to freedom of expression has been tested over and over again. Especially during times of national stress, like war abroad or social upheaval at home, people exercising their First Amendment rights have been censored, fined, even jailed. Those with unpopular political ideas have always borne the brunt of government repression. It was during WWI—hardly ancient history—that a person could be jailed just for giving out anti-war leaflets. Out of those early cases, modern First Amendment law evolved. Many struggles and many cases later, ours is the most speech-protective country in the world.

The path to freedom was long and arduous. It took nearly 200 years to establish firm constitutional limits on the government's power to punish "seditious" and "subversive" speech. Many people suffered along the way, such as labor leader Eugene V. Debs, who was sentenced to 10 years in prison under the Espionage Act just for telling a rally of peaceful workers to realize they were "fit for something better than slavery and cannon fodder." Or Sidney Street, jailed in 1969 for burning an American flag on a Harlem street corner to protest the shooting of civil rights figure James Meredith.

Free speech rights still need constant, vigilant protection. New questions arise and old ones return. Should flag burning be a crime? What about government or private censorship of works of art that touch on sensitive issues like religion or sexuality? Should the Internet be subject to any form of government control? What about punishing college students who espouse racist or sexist opinions? In answering these questions, the history and the core values of the First Amendment should be our guide.

## The Supreme Court and the First Amendment

During our nation's early era, the courts were almost universally hostile to political minorities' First Amendment rights; free speech issues did not even reach the Supreme Court until 1919 when, in *Schenck v. U.S.*, the Court unanimously upheld the conviction of a Socialist Party member for mailing anti-war leaflets to draft-age men. A turning point occurred a few months later in *Abrams v. U.S.* Although the

*The two dissenting opinions of Supreme Court justices Oliver Wendell Holmes, left, and Louis D. Brandeis in* Abrams v. U.S. *form the cornerstone of our First Amendment rights.*

defendant's conviction under the Espionage Act for distributing anti-war leaflets was upheld, two dissenting opinions formed the cornerstone of our modern First Amendment law. Justices Oliver Wendell Holmes and Louis D. Brandeis argued speech could *only* be punished *if* it presented "a clear and present danger" of imminent harm. Mere political advocacy, they said, was protected by the First Amendment. Eventually, these justices were able to convince a majority of the Court to adopt the "clear and present danger test."

From then on, the right to freedom of expression grew more secure—until the 1950s and McCarthyism. The Supreme Court fell prey to the witchhunt mentality of that period, seriously weakening the "clear and present danger" test by holding that speakers could be punished if they advocated overthrowing the government—even if the danger of such an occurrence were both slight and remote. As a result, many political activists were prosecuted and jailed simply for advocating communist revolution. Loyalty oath requirements for government employees were upheld; thousands of Americans lost their jobs on the basis of flimsy evidence supplied by secret witnesses.

Finally, in 1969, in *Brandenberg v. Ohio,* the Supreme Court struck down the conviction of a Ku Klux Klan member, and established a new standard: Speech can be suppressed only if it is intended, *and likely to produce,* "imminent lawless action." Otherwise, even speech that advocates violence is protected. The Brandenberg standard prevails today.

## Protected Speech

First Amendment protection is not limited to "pure speech"—books, newspapers, leaflets, and rallies. It also protects "symbolic speech"—nonverbal expression whose purpose is to communicate ideas. In its 1969 decision in *Tinker v. Des Moines,* the Court recognized the right of public school students to wear black armbands in protest of the

Vietnam War. In 1989 (*Texas v. Johnson*) and again in 1990 (*U.S. v. Eichman*), the Court struck down government bans on "flag desecration." Other examples of protected symbolic speech include works of art, T-shirt slogans, political buttons, music lyrics and theatrical performances.

Government can limit some protected speech by imposing "time, place and manner" restrictions. This is most commonly done by requiring permits for meetings, rallies and demonstrations. But a permit cannot be unreasonably withheld, nor can it be denied based on content of the speech. That would be what is called viewpoint discrimination—and *that* is unconstitutional.

When a protest crosses the line from speech to action, the government can intervene more aggressively. Political protesters have the right to picket, to distribute literature, to chant and to engage passersby in debate. But they do not have the right to block building entrances or to physically harass people.

## Hate Speech

The ACLU [American Civil Liberties Union] has often been at the center of controversy for defending the free speech rights of groups that spew hate, such as the Ku Klux Klan and the Nazis. But if only popular ideas were protected, we wouldn't need a First Amendment. History teaches that the first target of government repression is never the last. If we do not come to the defense of the free speech rights of the most unpopular among us, even if their views are antithetical to the very freedom the First Amendment stands for, then no one's liberty will be secure. In that sense, all First Amendment rights are "indivisible."

Censoring so-called hate speech also runs counter to the long-term interests of the most frequent victims of hate: racial, ethnic, religious and sexual minorities. We should not give the government the power to decide which opinions are hateful, for history has taught us that government is more apt to use this power to prosecute minorities than to protect them. As one federal judge has put it, tolerating hateful speech is "the best protection we have against any Nazi-type regime in this country."

At the same time, freedom of speech does not prevent punishing conduct that intimidates, harasses, or threatens another person, even if words are used. Threatening phone calls, for example, are not constitutionally protected.

## Speech and National Security

The Supreme Court has recognized the government's interest in keeping some information secret, such as wartime troop deployments. But the Court has never actually upheld an injunction against speech on national security grounds. Two lessons can be learned from this historical fact. First, the amount of speech that can be curtailed in the interest of national security is very limited. And second, the government has historically overused the concept of "national security" to shield itself from criticism, and to discourage public discussion of controversial policies or decisions.

In 1971, the publication of the "Pentagon Papers" by the *New York Times* brought the conflicting claims of free speech and national security to a head. The Pentagon Papers, a voluminous secret history and analysis of the country's involvement in Vietnam, was leaked to the press. When the *Times* ignored the government's demand that it cease publication, the stage was set for a Supreme Court decision. In the landmark *U.S. v. New York Times* case, the Court ruled that the government could not, through "prior restraint," block publication of any material unless it could prove that it would "surely" result in "direct, immediate, and irreparable" harm to the nation. This the government failed to prove, and the public was given access to vital information about an issue of enormous importance.

The public's First Amendment "right to know" is essential to its ability to fully participate in democratic decision-making. As the Pentagon Papers case demonstrates, the government's claims of "national security" must always be closely scrutinized to make sure they are valid.

## Unprotected Expression

The Supreme Court has recognized several limited exceptions to First Amendment protection.

In *Chaplinsky v. New Hampshire* (1942), the Court held that so-called "fighting words . . . which by their very utterance inflict injury or tend to incite an immediate breach of the peace," are not protected.

# Americans' Views on the First Amendment, 2008

*Based on your own feelings about the First Amendment, please say whether you agree or disagree with the following statement:*

**The First Amendment goes too far in the rights that it guarantees:**

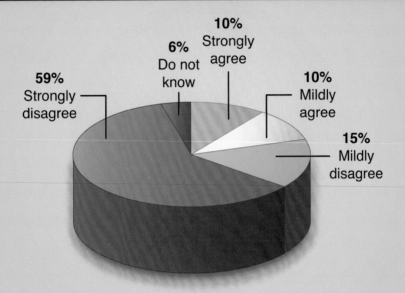

**10%** Strongly agree

**6%** Do not know

**59%** Strongly disagree

**10%** Mildly agree

**15%** Mildly disagree

Taken from: First Amendment Center, "State of the First Amendment 2008" (interviews conducted July 23–August 3, 2008). www.firstamendmentcenter.org.

This decision was based on the fact that fighting words are of "slight social value as a step to truth."

In *New York Times Co. v. Sullivan* (1964), the Court held that defamatory falsehoods about public officials can be punished—*only* if the offended official can prove the falsehoods were published with "actual malice," i.e. [that is]: "knowledge that the statement was false or with reckless disregard of whether it was false or not." Other kinds of "libelous statements" are also punishable.

Legally "obscene" material has historically been excluded from First Amendment protection. Unfortunately, the relatively narrow obscenity exception, described below, has been abused by government authorities and private pressure groups. Sexual expression in art and entertainment is, and has historically been, the most frequent target of censorship crusades, from James Joyce's classic *Ulysses* to the photographs of [artist] Robert Mapplethorpe.

In the 1973 *Miller v. California* decision, the Court established three conditions that must be present if a work is to be deemed "legally obscene." It must 1) appeal to the average person's prurient (shameful, morbid) interest in sex; 2) depict sexual conduct in a "patently offensive way" as defined by community standards; and 3) taken as a whole, lack serious literary, artistic, political or scientific value. Attempts to apply the "Miller test" have demonstrated the impossibility of formulating a precise definition of obscenity. Justice Potter Stewart once delivered a famous one-liner on the subject: "I know it when I see it." But the fact is, the obscenity exception to the First Amendment is highly subjective and practically invites government abuse.

## EVALUATING THE AUTHORS' ARGUMENTS:

In this viewpoint the American Civil Liberties Union (ACLU) identifies few areas of exceptions for protecting freedom of speech. Regarding the importance of protection, name one particular kind of speech that the ACLU and the author of the previous viewpoint, Goldberg, would appear to disagree on.

**Viewpoint**

**3**

# Flag Destruction Is Speech That Should Be Protected

## Cathy Young

*"The amendment against flag desecration is not only pointless, it's also pernicious."*

In the following viewpoint Cathy Young argues that a constitutional amendment to ban burning of the American flag is a bad idea. Young first notes that no evidence supports the notion that flag burning is a widespread problem. Second, Young contends that banning flag burning because it is offensive to many would leave the door open for censoring all kinds of symbolic speech that people find offensive. Young concludes that the irony of trying to ban destruction of this symbol is that if such censorship occurred, the importance of the symbol itself would be undermined. Young is an author and public speaker, a columnist for the *Boston Globe*, and a contributing editor at *Reason* magazine.

**AS YOU READ, CONSIDER THE FOLLOWING QUESTIONS:**

1. According to Young, in what year did the U.S. Supreme Court determine that burning the American flag was constitutionally protected free speech?

Cathy Young, "Abusing the Flag," *Boston Globe*, June 27, 2005. Copyright © 2005 Globe Newspaper Company. Reproduced by permission.

2. The First Amendment allows displays of what two offensive symbols, according to the author?
3. Young worries that in protecting the flag we might destroy what value that it symbolizes?

Just when you thought the political circus in Washington couldn't get any more grotesque, the politicos throw us a piece of pseudo-patriotic red meat: a constitutional amendment to prohibit the burning of the American flag, which was approved by the House last week [June 22, 2005,] and is now headed to the Senate.[1]

## Obscene Politicking

The anti-flag-desecration amendment has been around for years—ever since the Supreme Court ruled [in *Texas v. Johnson*], in 1989, that burning the flag was a form of constitutionally protected free speech. Previous attempts have failed to garner enough votes in the Senate. This time, with the Senate's more conservative make-up, the amendment has a better chance. If passed by the Senate, it would still have to be ratified by [three-fourths] of the states to become law.

Support for the amendment has always been a cheap ticket to political grandstanding. This time, though, it has been made worse by shameless exploitation of the memory of the victims of the Sept. 11, 2001, terrorist attacks. "Ask the men and women who stood on top of the Trade Center," Republican Representative Randy Cunningham of California declared during the House debate. "Ask them and they will tell you: Pass this amendment."

> ## FAST FACT
>
> The U.S. Supreme Court determined that defacing or destroying a flag is an act of protected speech under the First Amendment to the U.S. Constitution, first in *Texas v. Johnson* (1989) and later in *United States v. Eichman* (1990).

1. This measure failed by one vote in 2006.

"Obscene" is not too strong a word for this. If the men and women who died in the World Trade Center could talk to us, I suspect they might be a little more concerned about whether their fellow citizens are any better protected from terrorism today than four years ago.

If there is an epidemic of politically motivated flag-burning in this country, it certainly isn't very visible. When I did a news database search, it yielded a number of articles about demonstrations abroad in which the US flag was burned, several stories about the lawful disposal of old flags by the American Legion, and one report on cemetery vandalism. It's not exactly—pardon the pun—a burning issue.

## Poll on Anti-Flag-Destruction Amendment

**Do you think the United States Constitution should or should not be amended to prohibit burning or desecrating the American flag?**

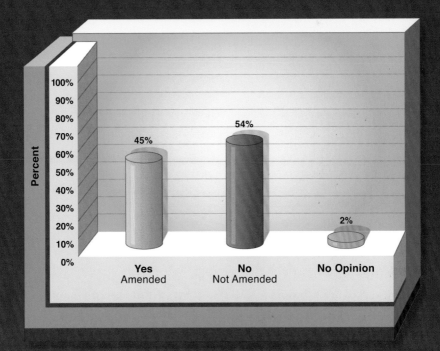

Taken from: Gallup poll, "Public Support for Constitutional Amendment on Flag Burning," June 29, 2006.*

*Poll conducted June 23–25, 2006. www.gallup.com.

*The U.S. Supreme Court ruled in 1989 that flag burning was protected under the First Amendment.*

The amendment against flag desecration is not only pointless, it's also pernicious. Yes, burning the flag is an offensive, outrageous, and stupid way to express your criticism of the US government. But the First Amendment says nothing about protecting only reasonable, polite, and intelligent speech. It protects speech, period—including nonviolent acts that are intended as statements. As conservatives like to remind liberals when it comes to hate speech directed at minorities, living in a free society means that sometimes you have to put up with your sensibilities being profoundly offended.

In a 2001 article in *The Los Angeles Times*, UCLA Law School professor Eugene Volokh draws an interesting analogy between the burning of the US flag and the flying of the Confederate flag. The Confederate flag, Volokh points out, is regarded by millions of Americans—particularly African-Americans—as an offensive symbol of racism and oppression. It can also be seen as a symbol of treason and rebellion against the US government. If we prohibit desecration of the US flag, why shouldn't the same logic lead us to prohibit displays of the Confederate flag? Asks Volokh, "What would we say when flag-burning is banned but other offensive symbols are allowed? We in the majority get to suppress symbols we hate, but you in the minority don't?"

Of course, the First Amendment allows the display of other, even more offensive symbols: the Nazi swastika, for instance, or the communist hammer and sickle. If we make it illegal to desecrate or maliciously destroy actual US flags, what about offensive displays of the image of the flag—for instance, a poster using visual symbols to equate the US flag with the swastika? Who decides, ultimately, what offensive expression can and cannot be regulated?

## A Symbol of Freedom

In 1989, after the Supreme Court ruling prompted the first cries for a constitutional amendment to ban flag-burning, *The Washington Post* published a remarkable piece by James H. Warner, a former Marine who spent six years as a prisoner of the North Vietnamese. He recalled an exchange with a communist interrogator who showed him a photo of American antiwar protesters burning a flag and told him that this proved his cause was wrong. Warner infuriated his interrogator by countering, "That proves that I am right. In my country we are not afraid of freedom, even if it means that people disagree with us."

Some say that the flag is different from all other symbols because it stands for our freedom. But how bitterly ironic it will be if, in protecting the symbol, we gut the freedom itself.

**EVALUATING THE AUTHOR'S ARGUMENTS:**

In this viewpoint Young contends that if we ban destruction of the flag, we would have to ban many other offensive symbols. In what way might a critic of her view argue that burning the flag is different from other kinds of speech that some find offensive?

# Flag Destruction Is Not Speech That Should Be Protected

*"Flag burning is not speech as defined by our Founding Fathers in the First Amendment."*

### The Citizens Flag Alliance

In the following viewpoint the Citizens Flag Alliance (CFA) argues that a right to destroy an American flag does not exist. The CFA contends that despite what the U.S. Supreme Court determined, the Constitution was never meant to protect flag burning as a form of free speech. The flag is an important national symbol, the CFA claims, and the importance of it warrants protecting it from destruction. The CFA is a nonpartisan, nonprofit, national organization that was formed to persuade Congress to pass a constitutional amendment that would give Congress the ability to ban flag desecration.

**AS YOU READ, CONSIDER THE FOLLOWING QUESTIONS:**

1. What 1989 U.S. Supreme Court decision took away the right of the people to protect the flag from destruction, according to the Citizens Flag Alliance (CFA)?

*Let the People Decide,* Indianapolis, IN: The Citizens Flag Alliance, 2008. Reproduced by permission.

2. According to the CFA, what percent of Congress believes that Americans have a right to protect their flag?
3. Citizens may purchase an American flag but ownership of the flag ultimately resides with whom, according to the CFA?

Forty-eight states and the federal government had flag-protection laws on the books during the summer of 1984 when Gregory Johnson (a leader of the Revolutionary Communist Youth Brigade) participated in an anti-America demonstration in Dallas, Texas. As the demonstrators marched from the site of the Republican National Convention to the steps of the Dallas City Hall, they defaced buildings with spray paint, turned over potted plants, stole an American flag from a Dallas bank, and generally made nuisances of themselves.

Then, as Texans watched in outrage and anger, Johnson torched the flag. While engaging in this offensive conduct, he chanted, "America, the red, white and blue . . . we spit on you." The Dallas police arrested Johnson. He was not arrested for anything he said about our government, our leaders, or our flag. He was arrested, charged, tried and convicted of desecration of a venerated object in violation of a Texas statute.

Five years later the U.S. Supreme Court heard the case. On June 21, 1989, in a 5–4 decision, the court ruled that Johnson had been denied his rights under the free speech provisions of the First Amendment. *Texas v. Johnson*, by one vote, took away the right of the people to protect the flag of our nation from intentional, public, physical desecration, a right we enjoyed since our birth as a nation. . . .

## Flag Burning Is Not Speech

Fiction: *Burning the American flag is protected "speech" as defined by the First Amendment to the Constitution.*

Fact: Flag burning is not speech as defined by our Founding Fathers in the First Amendment, which reads: "Congress shall make no law respecting an establishment of religion, or prohibiting the free exercise thereof; or abridging the freedom of speech, or of the press; or the right of the people peaceably to assemble, and to petition the Government for a redress of grievances."

James Madison, who wrote the First Amendment, condemned flag burning as a crime. Thomas Jefferson agreed with Madison and made clear in his writings that "speech" in the First Amendment meant the spoken word, not expressive conduct. To say otherwise made freedom "of the press" a redundancy. In fact, the words "expression" and "expressive conduct" are not in the Bill of Rights, and for good reason. Activist judges have added them to the Constitution in order to promote their own political agenda.

Since our birth as a nation, we the people have exercised our right to protect our flag. This right has been confirmed by every Chief Justice of the United States and Justices on five Courts in the last century who denied that flag burning was "speech." This fact is also confirmed by current constitutional experts, 70 percent of the Congress, the legislatures of all 50 states and more than three out of four Americans. . . .

## Protecting the Constitution

Fiction: *Flag burnings are rare and not important enough to justify changing the Constitution to punish a few miscreants.*

Fact: First, there have been hundreds of flag desecrations since the Supreme Court's 1989 decision. Second, the flag amendment does not change the Constitution, but restores it. In America the frequency of an evil has nothing to do with laws against that evil.

> # FAST FACT
>
> The Flag Protection Act of 1989, passed in response to the Supreme Court decision in *Texas v. Johnson* (1989) finding flag burning to be protected speech, was ruled unconstitutional a year later in *United States v. Eichman* (1990).

Shouting "fire" in a crowded theater or speaking of weapons in an airport are rare occurrences, but we have laws against them and we should. It is important to understand that those who would restore the right of the people to protect the flag are not concerned with punishing miscreants who desecrate it. They are not the problem. The problem is from those miscreants who desecrate the Constitution by calling flag burning "speech." We are not amending the Constitution only to protect the flag. We are doing it primarily to protect the Constitution.

*A member of the Citizens Flag Alliance attends a Kentucky rally promoting an amendment to the Constitution that would make flag burning illegal.*

## The Flag and Private Property

Fiction: *If the flag is my property, I can do with it as I wish as with any of my property.*

Fact: There are so many governmental restrictions on private property that one can't even formulate a general rule about private property. For instance, you can own your automobile, but how you use it is strictly regulated. Most states even require that you have periodic safety inspections, pay property taxes on it, and wear a seatbelt when operating it. The same is true for privately owned firearms and controlled drugs.

You can own the lot that your home sets on, but you can't use the property for any purpose you want that doesn't comply with zoning ordinances. The same is true for U.S. currency, your own mailbox, and military uniforms and decorations. You can own a billboard, but what you can display on it is regulated. And the same is true with the flag. Justice Byron White said each flag is the property of all the people. Our society has always believed that a citizen could purchase a flag, but ownership remained with the people. And possession of a flag carried with it a responsibility or duty to treat it with dignity and respect.

## The Flag and Its Representations
Fiction: *It is impossible to enforce flag protection, as it is impossible to legally define "desecration" or "flag."*

Fact: For most of our history we have had laws defining flag desecration and our courts had no problem until the Supreme Court misdefined flag desecration as "speech." Any fifth grade child knows the difference between an American flag and a flag-embroidered bikini or toilet paper with a printed flag replica.

For those who feign concern over prosecution for burning flag-marked bikinis or toilet paper, and can't discern the two from a flag, we ask: Would you put toilet paper or a bikini on the coffin of a veteran or [your] own coffin, or raise them from a flagpole during retreat? This is not only a non-issue, it is nonsense.

## The Flag as Symbol
Fiction: *The flag symbolizes my freedom to burn it.*

Fact: On the one hand they are saying the flag is a rag to be burned with impunity. And on the other hand they are saying it represents our freedoms. Can't have it both ways. The truth is our flag embodies the values embedded in our Constitution. The word "symbol" is from the Greek word meaning a half-token, which when united with its other half identified the owner. It is meant to recognize something

# Congressional Vote on Flag Desecration Amendment, 109th Congress

Text of the Amendment:

**"The Congress shall have power to prohibit the physical desecration of the flag of the United States."**

**House of Representative (June 22, 2005):**

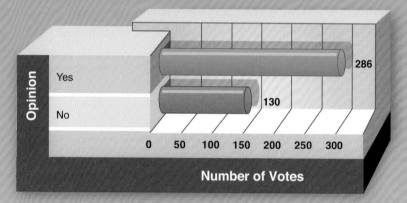

**Senate (June 27, 2006):**

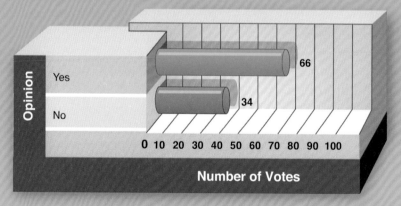

In order to be added to the Constitution, the amendment must be approved by a two-thirds vote of those present and voting in the Senate and House of Representatives, as well as be ratified by at least three-fourths of the fifty state legislatures. The 2005 vote succeeded in the House, but the 2006 vote failed in the Senate by one vote.

far more elaborate than itself. The other half of the token of the flag is the Constitution and it identifies its owners, the people. There is nothing in the Constitution that authorizes flag burning and the people are fighting to defeat this fiction.

More Medals of Honor, our nation's highest military award, have been awarded for flag protection than for any other act. Some actually died just to keep the flag from touching the ground. Are those who propose this fiction saying that our soldiers who died on America's battlefields to keep dictators and tyrants from defiling our flag did so in order that it could be burned on the streets of America? Who would say this to our warriors?

Supreme Court Justice Felix Frankfurter said, "We live by symbols." Symbols are vital in a democracy. How can one separate ideals from the symbols that house them? It is like separating a person from his soul. Symbols are precious in our lives and our country and all our precious symbols are protected, except our most precious symbol—Old Glory.

## EVALUATING THE AUTHORS' ARGUMENTS:

In this viewpoint the Citizens Flag Alliance argues that protecting symbols such as the flag is important to protecting the ideals they uphold. In what way would Cathy Young, author of the previous viewpoint, disagree with this?

**Viewpoint**

**5**

# Hate Speech Sometimes Warrants Censorship

*"Many of the nations where these cartoons [of the prophet Muhammad] have been published have laws against anti-Semitism— and rightly so."*

### Faisal Kutty

In the following viewpoint Faisal Kutty argues that not all speech should be protected. Kutty discusses the 2005 publication of cartoons depicting the prophet Muhammad in Denmark and elsewhere that many Muslims found offensive. Kutty claims that when speech promotes hate, the government should sometimes censor it, noting several countries that have laws forbidding such speech. Faisal Kutty is a lawyer with the Toronto-based firm KSM Law. He is also a visiting assistant professor of law at Valparaiso University School of Law and serves as an adjunct professor of law at Osgoode Hall Law School of York University.

AS YOU READ, CONSIDER THE FOLLOWING QUESTIONS:

1. The author discusses cartoons published in what Danish newspaper that led to a worldwide free speech debate?
2. Canada's Criminal Code forbids what type of statements, according to Kutty?
3. In noting the importance of the context of speech, Kutty claims that the original cartoons he discusses were published against a backdrop of what?

Faisal Kutty, "Danish Cartoons: Free Speech or Hate Speech?" *Catholic New Times,* March 19, 2006. Reproduced by permission.

"**I** don't know of anything more important than freedom of expression," said former [Canadian] Supreme Court Justice Peter Cory, when commenting on the Court's 1991 decision to uphold Jim Keegstra's conviction for willfully promoting hatred against Jews.

## Free Speech Battle

The offensive cartoons of the Prophet Muhammad originally published [September 30, 2005,] by the Danish newspaper, *Jyllands-Posten*, have now ignited global interest in the subject. Despite death and destruction, some free speech advocates have characterized this as a defining battle. It has now become a clash of extremes with both sides reeking of double standards. Muslim extremists—some of whom regularly insult others—and dictatorships are trying to claim the moral high ground by defending the sacred in clearly non-sacred ways. An equally hypocritical extreme in the West is pretending there are no limits and that subjective restraint is not exercised daily.

Four media outlets [in Canada], in addition to a student newspaper, have entered the fray, publishing or promising to show the controversial cartoons. The extreme right wing magazine, the *Western Standard*, and the *Jewish Free Press* ostensibly showed support for press freedoms. As well, TVO [TV Ontario] and the Quebec daily *Le Devoir* used the cartoons in the context of explaining the controversy.

There have been at least half-a-dozen protests throughout Canada. More than 4,000 people attended a peaceful rally at Toronto's Queen's Park on Feb. 19 [2006]. The Canadian Islamic Congress and the Islamic Supreme Council of Canada also filed complaints against the *Western Standard* and the *Jewish Free Press*, under the Criminal Code and human rights legislation.

## Laws Against Hate Speech

Many of the nations where these cartoons have been published have laws against anti-Semitism—and rightly so. In fact, Italian prosecutors recently announced charges against eleven individuals who displayed Nazi symbols during a football game. Meanwhile, media in Italy have reproduced the cartoons with impunity.

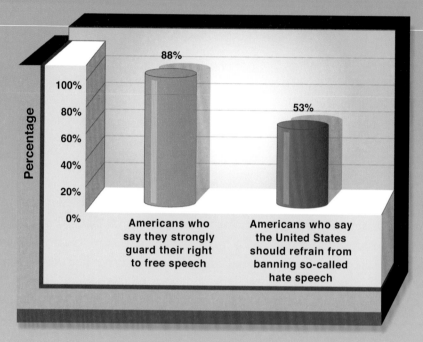

## The American Public Weighs In on Free Speech and Hate Speech

**88%**

**53%**

Percentage

100%
80%
60%
40%
20%
0%

Americans who say they strongly guard their right to free speech

Americans who say the United States should refrain from banning so-called hate speech

Taken from: Rasmussen Reports, "88% Say Free Speech Is Good, but Only 53% Oppose Ban on Hate Speech," June 16, 2008. www.rasmussenreports.com.

Denmark, too, has limits. Its laws prohibit blasphemy and expressions that threaten, deride or degrade others on various grounds. The offending newspaper, *Jyllands-Posten*, even refused to publish caricatures of Jesus in 2003 because they would "offend." Of course, these limits and laws are viewed through a political, social and philosophical lens. As a result, a public prosecutor came to the conclusion that the Danish cartoons did not violate any laws.

Freedom of expression is alive and well in Canada, but cannot be used as a carte blanche. We have restrictions. We have libel laws and censorship of various forms in keeping with "community standards." Moreover, criminal and human rights legislation also restrict free speech in the interest of protecting minorities and maintaining harmony.

Canada's Criminal Code proscribes statements that incite or promote hate. Convictions have been few and far between because of the specific intent required, but it has withstood constitutional challenges. Under Canadian law, it is an offence to incite "hatred against any identifiable group where such incitement is likely to lead to a breach of the peace." To be convicted, an accused must have communicated statements in a public place and ought to have known that the incitement was likely to have brought about a breach of the peace.

## Speech in Context

Though it can be argued that the cartoons, in and of themselves, may not be caught under law, there are strong grounds to lay a charge against those who republish them now. The news value has now diminished. Secondly, at least two of the cartoons, especially the one showing the prophet with the bomb and the one calling for an end to suicide bombings because of a shortage of virgins, suggest that Muslims are necessarily and inherently evil (this is a reasonable interpretation), because a Muslim by definition tries to emulate the prophet. The issue for most is not whether the prophet should be pictured. It is his portrayal, essentially, as a poster boy for al-Qaeda and by extension, Muslims in general, as violent and therefore worthy of hate.

Thirdly, given the fact that Muslims, both observant and non-observant, have made it very clear that these are offensive and violate their dignity as a community (granted this is an alien notion in our individualistic society), republishing them is therefore intentionally provocative and can promote hatred. As well, it can be reasonably argued that the intent behind their publication in the current climate will serve no real free speech purpose and may in fact expose Muslims to hate.

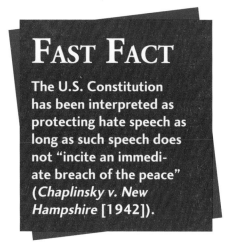

**FAST FACT**

The U.S. Constitution has been interpreted as protecting hate speech as long as such speech does not "incite an immediate breach of the peace" (*Chaplinsky v. New Hampshire* [1942]).

Lastly, I believe that the full context of its initial publication can shed some light on the intent behind its continued publication. They were published against a backdrop of ever increasing levels of Islamophobia and racism, where even the Queen of the land had called for the demonization of Muslims.

*The publication of cartoons of the Prophet Muhammad by a Danish newspaper sparked worldwide Muslim protests.*

The following quote from the South African newspaper the *Mail & Guardian* is illustrative: "Further, they were published in Denmark, which has been named by the European Union Commission on Human Rights as the most racist country in Europe. It has witnessed a large number of attacks against Muslims, some resulting in the killings of Muslim immigrants. And, they were published by a newspaper with historical ties to German and Italian fascism and which called for a fascist dictatorship in Denmark. *Jyllands-Posten* is also anti-immigrant and anti-Muslim. Within such a context, these cartoons are clearly hate speech. Their publication is an ontological attack against the foundations of Islam."

Indeed, some commentators have argued that given the foregoing, the aim of the cartoons was nothing short of inciting hatred against "the terrorist within." Nonetheless, Muslims in Canada have protested responsibly. Editors in the country must reciprocate and exercise their rights tempered by civic responsibility. The community will also be looking to the attorney general to enforce the laws against those who cross the line, joining the bandwagon of hate in the name of freedom of expression. As Justice Cory pointed out more than 15 years ago, laws against hate were justified because inciting hatred can be "as damaging as actual physical violence."

"Limits on free speech," said the justice, "must be considered as much as the right itself."

Amen.

## EVALUATING THE AUTHOR'S ARGUMENTS:

In this viewpoint Kutty suggests that with certain speech that is hateful or offensive, editors of publications should exercise responsibility or official action should be taken to stop the speech. Given what he says, do you think Kutty would advocate that publications refrain from publishing any religious cartoons that may be offensive?

# Self-Censorship of Offensive Speech Is Cowardly and Dangerous

**Doug Marlette**

*"In effect, we have capitulated to intimidation and threats and negotiated with terrorists."*

In the following viewpoint Doug Marlette argues that the reaction to the publication of cartoons offensive to many Muslims was overwhelmingly that of cowardice. Marlette criticizes the American media and famous artists for caving in to fear by not standing up for the rights of cartoonists to express politically sensitive material. Marlette contends that it is the role of political cartoons to provoke. He compares the critics of the cartoons who called for more responsible behavior on the part of cartoonists and publishers to those who criticized the work of Martin Luther King Jr. Marlette is a columnist and syndicated cartoonist, known for his editorial cartoons and his comic strip *Kudzu*.

Doug Marlette, "Them Damn Pictures," *Salon*, February 24, 2006. This article first appeared in Salon.com, at http://www.salon.com. An online version remains in the Salon archives. Reprinted with permission.

AS YOU READ, CONSIDER THE FOLLOWING QUESTIONS:
  1. According to Marlette, the incendiary cartoons should have been republished in America because of an obligation under what constitutional amendment?
  2. What explanation does the author give for the reluctance of newspaper cartoonists to stick their necks out in the cartoon debate?
  3. What does Marlette identify as the Japanese word for cartoon?

"Give up the cartoonists; they're in the attic." That is what many of us in the trade feel has been our lot since our brethren in Denmark were forced into hiding after drawing likenesses of the Prophet Mohammed. As art will do, "them damn pictures"—[nineteenth-century politician] Boss Tweed's term for Thomas Nast's cartoons from a more innocent time—have exposed not just the internal dynamics of what some have called Islamofascism but the corresponding corruption of our own values and character in the West. Our insides have been illuminated like an electrocuted Daffy Duck in an old Warner Brothers cartoon. And we now see what we're made of: not a lot of guts, or brains either.

## Reaction to the Cartoons

Admittedly, there's something about cartoons, which are by definition unruly, tasteless and immature, that brings out, if not the ayatollah [high-ranking Shiite religious leader], at least the disapproving parent in even the most permissive of adults. And granted, there may be a rights vs. responsibilities debate to be had over the Danish newspaper *Jyllands-Posten*'s original decision to commission images of Mohammed. But once these images became a major news story (and given that they easily satisfied Western standards of legitimate commentary and in fact only became internationally controversial after being misrepresented to the larger Muslim world) I can see little reason—other than bodily fear, bottom-line self-preservation, and just poor judgment—that the U.S. media and the public officials entrusted with defending our freedoms wimped out so thoroughly when challenged to live up to their historic obligation under the First

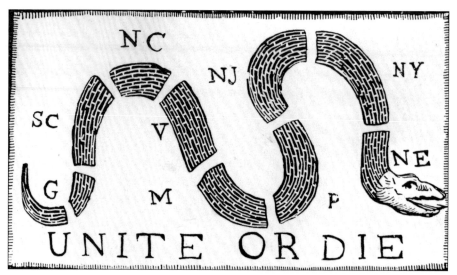

*The first "political cartoon" published in the United States was Ben Franklin's "Unite or Die" cartoon published in 1770.*

Amendment to keep the American public informed. When we withhold information in the name of a misguided sensitivity, by default we allow nihilistic street mobs from London to Jakarta to define the debate in this country. In effect, we have capitulated to intimidation and threats and negotiated with terrorists. No need for [Jordanian militant Islamist Abu Musab al-] Zarqawi to behead us. We do it ourselves.

Defensiveness about caving in to the imams [Islamic religious leaders] spread across the nation's editorial pages, while the 24-hour cable news talking heads clucked tongues about the irresponsible European press that had reprinted the offending images. Even cartoonist Garry Trudeau assured the *San Francisco Chronicle* that he would never depict the Prophet in his comics in a mocking way; nor would he show improper pictures of Jesus. As "Doonesbury's" Zonker might say, "Dude, this is so not about you!"

The images of Mohammed commissioned by *Jyllands-Posten* do not mock the Prophet any more than I dishonored Jesus Christ when I drew a cartoon of the Last Supper where Welch's grape juice was served. I was exposing the followers of Christ who used the doctrine of inerrancy to promote a crude agenda; the Danish cartoonists were not only exploring issues of self-censorship and intimidation but also depicting the hijacking of Islam by fanatics like the tormenters of [author] Salman Rushdie and the murderers of filmmaker Theo van Gogh. I would further argue that publishing those cartoons was an act of democratic inclusiveness. In a society of laws, all are treated equally under the law. Law is "insensitive" that way, as is intellectual inquiry, as is satire. By engaging satirically with Islam, these brave artists included Muslims as peers in the tradition of satiric self-examination and irreverence that we have until recently taken for granted in the West. And Denmark's Muslims might have simply expressed their displeasure through the accepted democratic avenues of their adopted country if their unscrupulous imams and the corrupt Arab governments whose tyranny they serve hadn't manipulated the cartoons (by, for example, disseminating some offensive drawings that were not part of the original, rather tame, Danish package) to ignite riots across the Muslim world.

## Cowardice in America

As newspapers in Europe and even Muslim editors in Jordan withstood the intimidation of the jihadists by reprinting the cartoons, the continuing timidity of the American media looks increasingly like cowardice, appeasement, or better-you-than-me cynicism. National spokespersons, meanwhile, have seconded the Muslim point of view; the public relations ambassador Karen Hughes compared the drawings to racial slurs, calling them "blasphemous," and former President [Bill] Clinton described them as "appalling." By denying their audiences the opportunity to decide for themselves by looking at the images, American media outlets, with few exceptions, kept the public in the dark about the roots of one of the year's major news stories. (Though actually, adding to the absurdity of the mainstream media's editorial anguish, the images are only a mouse click away on the Internet.) The press's reticence is not going to make this controversy go away, any more than its ignoring the newly released images out of Abu Ghraib [the notorious prison in Baghdad where Iraqi prisoners were tortured by American soldiers] will make them hate us any less in the Arab world.

We expect such bad thinking and Dilbertism from the corporate media culture, but when artists fear for their lives because of something they've drawn, where are the defenders of free expression among their fellow artists in this country? I understand why newspaper cartoonists, who have seen their jobs shrink from more than 200 only 20 years ago to fewer than 80 today, are reluctant to stick their necks out. Hence, no special day sponsored by the American Association of Editorial Cartoonists designated to drawing the Prophet Mohammed or, failing that, turning in blank cartoons in solidarity with our fellow Danish artists in hiding. But what about those artists who enjoy the immunity of celebrity? Earth to Barbra Streisand. Earth to Alec Baldwin.

## The Nature of Political Cartoons

I first got a whiff of the cosmic ramifications of this story last December when the culture editor of *Jyllands-Posten* contacted me for an interview about the threats I had received after drawing an Arab driving a Ryder Truck loaded with a nuke (this was in 2002, before Iran) under the caption "What Would Mohammed Drive?" Though this cartoon was more inflammatory than any of the ones that have caused riots around the world, I was merely denounced on the front page of the *Saudi Arab News* by the secretary general of the Muslim World League, and my newspaper, syndicate and home computer were flamed with tens of thousands of e-mails, viruses and death threats aimed at intimidating my publishers and shutting me up.

Still, this was a bit more excitement than I had in mind when I addressed the first East-West journalism conference, held in Prague, in July 1990, about the incendiary role of the cartoonist. I explained to the freshly minted free press there about how the American cartoon was born in revolution. (The very first, designed by Ben Franklin, showed a snake cut into eight segments, each representing one of the colonies. The legend read "Unite or Die.") The best political cartoons, I told them, are always created in the spirit of the Prague Spring and the Velvet Revolution. They question authority, challenge the status

## FAST FACT

After publication of controversial cartoons in the Danish newspaper *Jyllands-Posten* on September 30, 2005, protests in the Muslim world led to attacks on Danish embassies in Syria, Lebanon, and Iran.

ARES.
caglecartoons.com/espanol

"The Cartoonist," cartoon by Best of Latin America and CagleCartoons.com, February 8, 2006. Copyright © 2006 by Best of Latin America, Ares and CagleCartoons.com. All rights reserved.

quo and are inevitably accused of "Disturbing the Peace," borrowing the title of one of Václav Havel's books. If the editorial cartoons are doing their job, efforts will be made to suppress them.

## The Notion of Responsibility

So that week in Prague, hearing the easterners repeatedly admonished to be "responsible in their journalism," I took the opportunity to point out that the Japanese word for cartoon is "irresponsible drawings." Responsibility, of course, like beauty, lies always in the eye of the beholder. The reporting of some of the great journalists present there at that conference—datelined Vietnam, for example—was often labeled "irresponsible." Václav Havel's writings were called "irresponsible" by the Soviet thought controllers who not long before had convened in the hotel where we were staying. The list of "irresponsible" expression goes on: from the *Washington Post*'s coverage of Watergate to the *New York Times*' revelations of warrantless wiretapping.

Having grown up in the Southern United States during the era of the civil rights movement, I remember how business, civic and religious leaders called Martin Luther King Jr. "irresponsible" as a way of disagreeing with his means without having to actually take a moral stand on his ends. Those cautioning "responsibility" in today's cartoon controversy—in both the West and the Middle East—have much in common with those "good people" of the segregated South, who preferred, as King wrote, "a negative peace which is the absence of tension to a positive peace which is the presence of justice." Their own decent, Christian values were embarrassed by terrorists who burned crosses and bombed churches in the name of Jesus, as Islam has been subverted by the hooded thugs of Muslim extremism. And like the politicians and oligarchs of the segregated South, the corrupt leadership of these Arab countries encourages the anti-cartoonists because their violent passions are a diversion from the government's own neglect and abuse of its people.

## Stand Up for the Cartoonists

Why haven't the true Muslims, moderate religionists, men and women of good will, risen up to condemn those who so disgrace their faith? We constantly ask this question even though the answer is contained in the reluctance of our own civilization's instruments of free expression to confront the problem. "Fill the jails" was Gandhi's strategy of non-cooperation with a non-democratic system, for making society look at right and wrong in a fresh way, and it was one that Martin Luther King adopted in 1963 when he flooded the jails of Birmingham to defeat segregation. I submit that just as that non-violent demonstration of solidarity and defiance exposed a corrosive political system and channeled the outrage of helplessness constructively, so would a form of cartoon direct action have advanced the true interests of Islam.

King wrote in his "Letter From a Birmingham Jail," "Actually, we who engage in nonviolent direct action are not the creators of tension. We merely bring to the surface the hidden tension that is already alive. We bring it out in the open, where it can be seen and dealt with."

Here's what the American media might have done and could still do in response to the cartoon riots. In the spiritually expansive style of Gandhi and King, they could summon their aggregate moral authority and humbly dedicate a page of their newspaper or half a minute of their newscasts to showing the cartoons and explaining why they must, not as a taunt but as a restatement of democratic principle, as a prayer for coexistence. If everyone had stood up for Denmark's embattled cartoonists, then the taboo images might have lost their meaning, as going to jail lost its stigma when it was in the service of freedom. Collecting his Nobel Peace Prize on the heels of the Birmingham campaign, King noted that "every crisis has both its dangers and its opportunities." Perhaps one day the *Jyllands-Posten* cartoonists will be recognized for their contributions to democratic health and a peace truer than the one they have disturbed.

**EVALUATING THE AUTHORS' ARGUMENTS:**

In this viewpoint Marlette argues that publishing cartoons critical of the Islamic world was an act of inclusiveness, subjecting Muslims to criticism just as cartoonists subject Christians and people of other faiths to criticism and commentary. Why might Faisal Kutty, author of the previous viewpoint, claim that in the current context, such similar treatment in the West is not inclusive?

# Chapter 2

# Can Censorship Be Justified as Protection for Children?

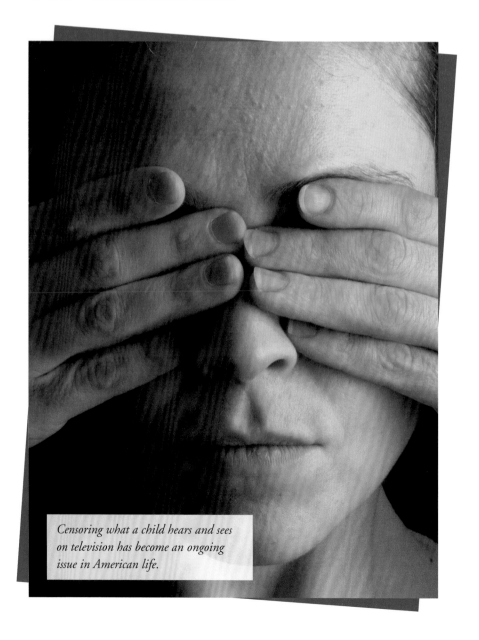

*Censoring what a child hears and sees on television has become an ongoing issue in American life.*

**Viewpoint**

**1**

# Decency Standards on Television Are Necessary to Protect Children

**Parents Television Council**

*"Parents who are concerned about TV's influence on impressionable children cannot just passively accept the current state of broadcast television."*

In the following viewpoint the Parents Television Council (PTC) reveals the results of its analysis of programs aired during the Family Hour on major network television stations, arguing that they contain too much objectionable content. The PTC contends that the levels of foul language, violence, and sexual content are high, with few shows having no objectionable content at all. The PTC contends that the problem is getting worse and that the entertainment industry needs to engage in self-regulation, or else government regulation will be necessary. The PTC is a nonpartisan education organization advocating responsible entertainment.

*The Alarming Family Hour . . . No Place for Children,* Los Angeles, CA: Parents Television Council, 2007.

**AS YOU READ, CONSIDER THE FOLLOWING QUESTIONS:**

1. According to the analysis by the Parents Television Council (PTC), what percent of the 208 episodes viewed during the Family Hour were free of violence, sexual content, and foul language?
2. What percent of programs contained violent content, according to the PTC's study?
3. The PTC cites a 2007 poll that shows what percent of people believe too much sex, violence, and coarse language is on television?

Traditionally known as the Family Hour, the first hour of prime time was once a place for programming the whole family could enjoy. Television broadcasters, exercising their corporate responsibility to act in the public interest, reserved adult-themed shows for later in the evening when the youngest viewers were likely to be asleep.

In recent years, however, the broadcast networks have pushed more and more adult-oriented programming to the early hours of the evening.

This Special Report constitutes the PTC's [Parents Television Council] sixth analysis of Family Hour programming. The study sample included all entertainment programs originally airing on the six major broadcast networks (ABC, CBS, Fox, NBC, CW, and My Network TV) in the Family Hour during three separate two-week periods of the 2006–2007 television season: November 2–15, 2006; February 1–14, 2007; and April 26–May 9, 2007.

## The Family Hour

The Family Hour time slot includes programs with a start time between 8 and 9 P.M. Monday through Saturday and between 7 and 9 P.M. on Sundays, in the Eastern time zone (7 to 8 P.M. Monday through Saturday, and 6 to 8 P.M. Sunday in the Central time zone).

Reruns were analyzed separately. Many of the programs that were rebroadcast during the Family Hour normally occupy a later time slot on the broadcast schedule and are intended for adult audiences. Thus, by airing them during the Family Hour, the networks are introducing young audiences to high levels of mature content.

In 180 hours of original programming, there were 2246 instances of objectionable violent, profane and sexual content, for an average of 12.48 instances per television hour, or one instance every 4.8 minutes. Since the average hour of prime-time broadcast television contains about 43 minutes of non-commercial programming, one instance of objectionable content occurs every 3.5 minutes of non-commercial airtime, on average. Only 10.6% of the 208 episodes were free of any violent and sexual content and foul language. CW was the cleanest network overall with 9.44 instances of objectionable content per hour. Fox was the worst network overall with 20.78 instances of objectionable content per hour.

The only shows with no objectionable content were game shows/reality competitions: *Deal or No Deal* (NBC), *Are You Smarter than a 5th Grader?* (Fox), *Identity* (NBC), and *Grease: You're the One That I Want* (NBC). *American Dad* (Fox), with 52 instances of objectionable content per hour, was the worst series of the Family Hour.

> ## FAST FACT
>
> The Federal Communications Commission (FCC) officially established a family viewing hour between 8 P.M. and 9 P.M. in 1975, but a circuit court judge in 1976 ruled that the policy was not binding.

## Foul Language, Sex, and Violence

There were 815 uses of foul language, or 4.53 per hour. More than ¾ of all programs airing in the Family Hour (76.4%) contained foul language. MyNetworkTV had the highest frequency of foul language with 5.58 instances per hour. The program with the highest rate of foul language was *My Name is Earl* (NBC) with 16.33 instances per hour.

There were 677 sexual scenes or spoken sexual references, an average of 3.76 per hour. Well over half of all programs (54.8%) contained sexual content. Since 2000–2001, the amount of sexual content during the Family Hour has increased by 22.1%. CBS experienced the largest increase in sexual content since 2000–2001, from

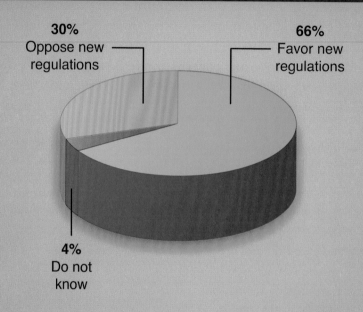

**Percent of parents who favor new regulations to limit the amount of sex and violence in television shows during the early evening hours:**

30%
Oppose new
regulations

66%
Favor new
regulations

4%
Do not
know

Taken from: The Henry J. Kaiser Family Foundation, "Parents, Children & Media: A Kaiser Family Foundation Survey," June 2007. www.kff.org.

0.34 to 2.31 instances per hour—a 579% increase. ABC had the most sexual content with 5.97 instances per hour. *The War at Home* (Fox) had the highest frequency of sexual content of any program with 33 instances per hour.

There were 754 violent acts and images, or 4.19 per hour. Nearly half of all programs (46.2%) contained violent content. Since 2000–2001, violent content has increased by 52.4%. Fox experienced the largest increase in violent content, going from 2.16 instances per hour in 2000–2001 to 11.37 per hour in 2006–2007—a 426% increase. Fox was also the worst network for violence, with 11.37 instances per hour. *24* (Fox) was the most violent non-animated series, with 28 instances of violence per hour.

In the three two-week periods, the networks aired 37.5 hours of reruns during the Family Hour containing an average of 19.76 instances of objectionable content per hour—58% more per hour than in original Family Hour programming. Reruns contained 80% higher rates of sexual content per hour than did original programming. Reruns contained over twice as much violence per hour as original programs.

## The Issue Is Worsening

At the time of our last comprehensive study of early evening programming in 2001, the PTC joined a bipartisan coalition in the U.S. Congress to call on the broadcast television industry to self-regulate in order to preserve at least one hour each night of family-friendly television. The initial response was somewhat encouraging, with advertisers and some of the networks announcing efforts to clean up the Family Hour.

Unfortunately that initial encouragement was short-lived. In the past six years [2001–2007], the Family Hour has become even more hostile to children and families. There is no safe haven for children on nightly broadcast television.

We found that the Family Hour has become increasingly laced with sex and violence. Along with scheduling adult-themed shows like *Bones* and *Desire* for the Family Hour, we also found the networks taking graphic and explicit shows that had originally run in later timeslots, like *Grey's Anatomy* and *C.S.I.*, and re-airing them during the Family Hour.

## The Need for Regulation

The American public is overwhelmingly concerned. In a March 2007 Zogby Poll, 79% of respondents agreed that there is too much sex, violence and coarse language on television. Other surveys have shown that parents are so fed up that they would welcome more government regulation to rein-in television content. However, through responsible self-regulation, the entertainment industry might eliminate the need for further legislative or regulatory action.

The broadcast networks, who are given access to a public resource, [that is] the broadcast airwaves, need to fulfill their public interest obligation by bringing back the Family Hour.

Advertisers need to do more to support positive, family-friendly programming during the early evening, committing their advertising dollars to clean shows, and exerting economic pressure on the broadcast networks to provide more family-friendly programming during the first hour of prime time.

The industry must provide parents with a meaningful ratings system, one that is accurate, consistent, and transparent and will adequately warn parents about potentially offensive content. This is especially important during the first hour of prime time when you have the largest number of children in the television viewing audience.

Parents who are concerned about TV's influence on impressionable children cannot just passively accept the current state of broadcast television. They must actively oppose the broadcast networks' efforts to obliterate decency standards by pressuring their local broadcast

*Tim Winter, left, president of the Parents Television Council, testifies along with noted academics before a Senate committee on violence in the media and television shows during Family Hour.*

affiliates to refuse to air programs containing high levels of inappropriate sex, violence and profanity during the Family Hour and by pressuring the advertisers to stop underwriting offensive Family Hour content.

**EVALUATING THE AUTHOR'S ARGUMENTS:**

In this viewpoint the Parents Television Council argues that less objectionable content should be on major broadcast television stations during certain times in the evening when children are likely to be watching. Name one other solution for concerned parents besides regulating television content.

# Parents, Not Decency Standards, Should Regulate Television

*"If parents are truly worried about their kids and TV, they will make more use of [filtering] technology in future."*

### Economist

In the following viewpoint the *Economist* argues that the time has come to eliminate laws against indecency on television. Despite calls from social conservatives to extend decency regulations, the *Economist* argues that changes in television and filtering technology make these rules obsolete. Parents now have the option to choose among hundreds of television stations, and technology allows them to block individual channels as well as individual programs—thus parents, not government, should be responsible for what their children watch. The *Economist* is a weekly newspaper that offers analyses of world business and current affairs.

AS YOU READ, CONSIDER THE FOLLOWING QUESTIONS:
1. According to the *Economist,* since what year has the Federal Communications Commission (FCC) tried to protect children from sexual content and profanity?
2. What fraction of American households subscribe to cable or satellite television, according to the author?
3. The *Economist* cites a recent survey that shows what percent of people believe that kids' parents are most responsible for screening TV shows for objectionable content?

A
merica's lawmakers should scrap, not extend, rules restricting "indecency" on television.

"We find that the fleeting uses of the words 'penis', 'vaginal', 'ass', 'bastard' and 'bitch', uttered in the context of the programs cited in the complaints, do not render the material patently offensive under contemporary community standards for the broadcast medium." Making decisions like this is one of the more thankless tasks of America's media regulator, the Federal Communications Commission. Since 1927 the FCC has tried to protect children from "indecency"—sexual content and swear words—on broadcast television and radio.

Under pressure from social conservatives, America's politicians are now threatening to extend indecency regulation further. If they get their way, not just broadcast television and radio but cable and satellite TV, and possibly satellite radio, would be monitored by the FCC for indecency. America's media firms have been shaken by this threat.

**FAST FACT**

The Federal Communications Commission (FCC) is the agency that enforces federal laws prohibiting obscene programming at any time and indecent programming or profane language during certain hours.

Every society, of course, has the right to protect children from adult material. But increasing censorship by the central government is the wrong way to go about this. A wiser course would be to eliminate the government's role and rely more on parents. Fortunately, changes in technology and the media industry itself now make this approach more feasible than ever.

Television has changed beyond recognition since indecency rules were first imposed. In 1978 the Supreme Court upheld the FCC's right to punish indecency on the grounds that broadcasters had what it called a "uniquely pervasive presence in the lives of all Americans." Back then, that was a plausible argument. But with television fragmenting into so many outlets such unique pervasiveness no longer prevails. Over four-fifths of American households, for instance, subscribe to cable or satellite television. They are just as likely to be watching one of the hundreds of cable channels they have at home as

*Lawrence Lien of Parental Guide, Inc., shows how the V-chip is used to block television programs containing sex, violence, and inappropriate language.*

The government currently has some authority to regulate content on broadcast television. Should that authority be extended to allow the regulation of programs available by subscription to cable or satellite television systems?

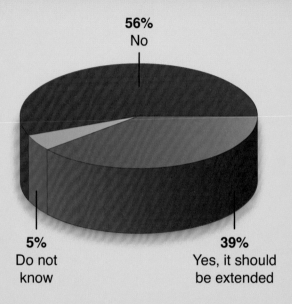

**56%**
No

**5%**
Do not
know

**39%**
Yes, it should
be extended

Taken from: First Amendment Center, "State of the First Amendment 2008," Interviews July 23–August 3, 2008.
www.firstamendmentcenter.org.

one of the main six broadcast networks. With so much choice, avoiding the indecent is easier than it was 30 years ago when most people had only three channels.

At the same time, new technology now allows families to filter the television they receive. Cable and satellite TV come with set-top boxes that can screen out individual channels. Digital cable set-top boxes are particularly precise, and allow parents to block individual programmes at the touch of a button on their remote control. Every new television set sold in America since 2000 is equipped with a

"V-chip", a blocking device that Bill Clinton forced on the media industry in 1996. It is only thanks to the V-chip and set-top boxes, in fact, that children get any protection from violence, since the FCC regulates only sex and bad language. America is the only country where blocking technology is already in the vast majority of homes, thanks to the ubiquity of pay television. But it is likely soon to be available elsewhere as well.

## Couch Potatoes

Many parents in America are either ignorant of the tools at their disposal or too busy or lazy to use them. But that is not a good enough reason to prolong the government's role. If parents are truly worried about their kids and TV, they will make more use of the technology in future. As a whole, Americans believe that responsibility lies with parents. The Pew Research Centre reported in March that 86% of the people it surveyed said that parents are most responsible for screening kids from sex and violence, and just 4% named the federal government.

That is not to say that the media industry should not do more to help parents protect their children. Media executives admit that they could do a better job of labelling programmes. It was only a few months ago that NBC, a broadcast network owned by General Electric, finally agreed to give its audience the full range of content ratings that the rest of the industry uses. But America's entertainment industry is now wide awake to the fact that, if it does not do everything it can to make the system work, it may face more direct regulation. In response, cable television firms have promised to spend $250m on ads to remind people that they have the tools to filter content themselves. Their other priority should be to ensure that their labelling system is reliable and consistent.

There is one strong argument against scrapping indecency regulation for television. Kids not lucky enough to have responsible parents might end up being exposed to more adult sex and profanity. But people should weigh the risk of that outcome against the harm of allowing each incoming administration to decide what everyone can and cannot watch. The current government has shown that it can easily broaden the country's definition of what is indecent. Under pressure from Congress, the FCC has cracked down and has overruled its own precedents. What might future governments do? Technology has offered the chance to scale back censorship and America, long a champion of free speech, should seize it.

## EVALUATING THE AUTHORS' ARGUMENTS:

In this viewpoint the *Economist* argues that parents, not government, should regulate children's television viewing. Do you think that the author of the previous viewpoint, the Parents Television Council (PTC), would be satisfied by the claim that parents can rely on filtering devices to eliminate objectionable programming? Why or why not?

# Parents Should Have a Say About Which Books End Up in Schools

## Warren Throckmorton

*"Schools should allow parents to have a clue about what their kids are exposed to."*

In the following viewpoint Warren Throckmorton argues that parents have legitimate concerns about the books their children are being exposed to in school—through classes and the library. Throckmorton claims that it is reasonable for parents to challenge schools with respect to the presence of certain books in the school. If the books are not removed, Throckmorton claims that it is perfectly acceptable for the school to be required to gain parental permission for any student exposure to these contested books. Throckmorton is an associate professor of psychology and a fellow for psychology and public policy at Grove City College in Pennsylvania. Concerned Women for America is a national organization devoted to bringing biblical principles into public policy.

Warren Throckmorton, "Should Raunchy Be the Fourth R?" Concerned Women for America, www.cwfa.org, August 18, 2005. Reproduced by permission.

**AS YOU READ, CONSIDER THE FOLLOWING QUESTIONS:**
1. Throckmorton claims that recent changes in children's literature and in society have focused the debates about school libraries on what sensitive subject?
2. The author describes how Laurie Taylor became concerned about school reading material; what did she ask librarians to do?
3. What does the author believe must happen if teachers want to use portions of contested books in class?

School is just around the corner. Awaiting anxious students are new schedules, new teachers, new challenges and in some school districts, old controversies about what books should be read in school. Wow, where did the summer go?

## Sex in Children's Literature

School districts have been facing decisions over what should be in the library as long as there have been libraries, but recent changes in the world of children's literature and our society have focused the debates on teen sexuality. A recent MSNBC article describes growing parental concern over the explicit nature of books aimed at young teens.

Correspondent Janet Shamlian reports on some recent hot selling teen titles:

> In *Claiming Georgia Tate*, a father has sex with his daughter. In *Rainbow Party*, teens make plans for an oral sex party. And in *Teach Me*, out next week and seemingly ripped from the day's headlines, there's a student-teacher affair.

While I am not aware of challenges to any of these specific books, there probably will be some if they find their way into schools. Recent disputes over books in Lexington, Massachusetts, Pleasant Valley, Iowa and Columbus, Ohio have divided communities and led to legal action.

Perhaps the mother of all of these disputes over school reading material is in Fayetteville, Arkansas. Laurie Taylor, a mother of two school-age children . . . , recently found numerous volumes of fiction

Tango Makes Three, *a book based on a true story about two male penguins that raise an adopted hatchling together, was banned by Charlotte-Mecklenburg schools in North Carolina after parent protests.*

that vividly describe sexual acts of all sorts. *Doing It* features teacher-pupil sex, *Rainbow Boys* describes adult-teen unprotected homosexual sex, and *Choke*, uncovering the world of sexaholics, was graphic enough to have portions excerpted in *Playboy*. Perhaps the worst find was *Push*, by author Sapphire. Filled with graphic sex, the book's low point is the lead character's description of sex with an infant.

## Challenges to Books

Mrs. Taylor is formally challenging these and other fiction books with similar content. While she believes that some books are not suitable for any ages and should be removed, she is asking that librarians gain parents' permission before allowing children to have access to others with questionable content. She also wants the school to follow its own review policy while parents mediate children's access. The Fayetteville district requires schools to review materials that parents find objectionable.

For these reasonable requests, she has been pilloried in the local press as narrow minded and bigoted. The school district has received a veiled threat of a lawsuit from national groups including the National Coalition Against Censorship, a front for pornography producers.

Is Mrs. Taylor overreacting? Should these books be in public school libraries? Before I throw in my view, let me jump back to the MSNBC article on racy teen novels. Reporter Shamlian writes: "Experts say books like these are gratuitous—even dangerous—and parents need to know that." She then quotes a specialist in adolescent psychiatry, Dr. John Sargent: "They buy it, thinking they're doing something nice for their kid, when, in fact, they have no clue what it is they're exposing their kid to."

## The Rights of Parents

I agree with Dr. Sargent. Such reading material can be counterproductive to a healthy view of sexuality. Some of these books normalize and even glamorize sexual behavior that most educators and parents would like to prevent. Surely there are other ways to provide an education on topics touched by these books. What should public schools do about such gratuitous material?

Where a review panel of parents and teachers cannot agree about the appropriateness of a contested book, parental permission should be required. If teachers want to use explicit portions of contested books, then parents should be notified. Schools should allow parents to have a clue about what their kids are exposed to. Such a policy does no violence to free speech, nor is it censorship. If some parents want raunchy to join readin', 'ritin' and 'rithmetic, they are free to buy their own children sexually explicit material for consumption at home.

**EVALUATING THE AUTHOR'S ARGUMENTS:**

In this viewpoint Throckmorton concludes that parental permission should be required when books at school are contested, and he claims that this policy does not violate free speech. How might a critic argue that this policy would violate the freedom of expression guaranteed by the First Amendment?

# Banning Books in Schools Promotes Ignorance and Intolerance

**Thomas G. Palaima**

*"Banning books and ideas promotes ignorance and intolerance."*

In the following viewpoint Thomas G. Palaima argues that banning books is dangerous, since books and ideas counteract ignorance and intolerance. Palaima believes that many people unwisely treat censorship lightly, unaware of the difficult fights waged against censorship in the past and the danger still posed by it. Palaima worries that attempting to censor certain books in schools will deprive students of the opportunity to examine serious issues. Palaima is the Raymond F. Dickson Centennial Professor of Classics and director of the Program in Aegean Scripts and Prehistory at the University of Texas at Austin. He is a regular contributor to the *Austin American-Statesman*.

Thomas G. Palaima, "A School's Wise Stand Against Book Banning," *Austin American-Statesman*, October 5, 2005. Reproduced by permission.

AS YOU READ, CONSIDER THE FOLLOWING QUESTIONS:
1. What quote by President Lyndon Baines Johnson does the author refer to in support of his view of the danger of banning books?
2. What are two of the books that the author identifies as having been banned in the past?
3. Palaima claims that works by what well-known Greek philosopher were banned in Greece from 1967 to 1976?

B anned Books Week, sponsored by the American Library Association, has come and gone so fast in Austin and at the University of Texas [UT] that it might have escaped your notice.

## The Dangers of Banning Books

A search of UT's main Web site shows only one event the entire week, Sept. 24 to Oct. 1 [2005], devoted to the topic of book banning— a two-hour discussion sponsored by the Student Association of the School of Information. Why such apathy at a major research university about such an important topic? Well, I am ashamed to say that Banned Books Week almost passed me by, despite the fact that the library association's Web site features an Austin connection. It quotes [former U.S. president] Lyndon Baines Johnson's [LBJ] belief that "books and ideas are the most effective weapons against intolerance and ignorance."

## FAST FACT

Banned Books Week (BBW), started in 1982, is an annual American Library Association (ALA) event during the last week of September that celebrates the freedom to read.

If you agree with LBJ, then it follows that banning books and ideas promotes ignorance and intolerance. Why, then, do we and other cultures throughout history censor what we read, hear, see and discuss? Part of the answer, of course, is that tolerance and truth lie in the eyes of the beholders. We all have different opinions about whether ideas are good or bad, helpful or harmful, and who should be exposed to them. Just these kinds of issues led me to find out about Banned Books Week in the first place.

St. Andrew's Episcopal School here in Austin recently made a hard but wise decision. It resisted the influence of $3 million and decided against a donor's wishes to ban the use of Pulitzer Prize–winner Annie Proulx's short story "Brokeback Mountain" in a 12th grade English class because of its gay sexual content. So I went out to find a copy of the offending work.

## The Foundation for Free Inquiry

If, like me, you went into Half-Price Books at Lamar Boulevard and Koenig Lane [in Austin, TX], you would have seen a prominent display of "hot reading"—books that have been banned in the past. The

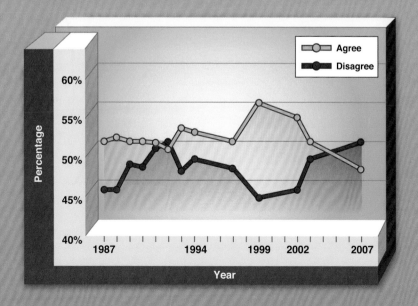

## Changing Views on Book Banning

Books that contain dangerous ideas should be banned from school and public libraries:

Taken from: Pew Research Center, "Trends in Political Values and Core Attitudes: 1987–2007," March 22, 2007. www.pewresearch.org.

*The Gadsen Public Library in Gadsen, Alabama, shows a Banned Books Week display to recognize the American Library Association's efforts to encourage readers to judge books not by their covers, but without them.*

display included Mark Twain's *Huckleberry Finn*, Toni Morrison's *Beloved*, Shakespeare's *Merchant of Venice*, D.H. Lawrence's *Women in Love*, James Joyce's *Ulysses*, Charles Darwin's *Origin of the Species* and the Greek comic poet Aristophanes' *Lysistrata*. It even had the Bible.

One reason for taking book censorship so lightly is how amusing it looks in retrospect, especially in our society, which at least in principle values openness and mutual understanding. It leads us to think that in time, people will come to their senses and reason will prevail. But this is a foolish way to think. The censorship documented in that book display was real, and it took personal courage and long, hard work to undo it.

Back in 1982 while at a conference in Prague, I stayed with a Czech family behind the Iron Curtain. Every night, the mother of the family stayed up reading a samiszdat [secretly produced controversial or banned literature] carbon-copy typed version of Leon Uris' novel *Exodus*, about the founding of Israel. She had a week to read this banned text and pass it on to someone else. For her, censorship was grim and repressive. Her teenage son wanted to play for me some contemporary folk music, but she cautioned against it.

Aristophanes' *Lysistrata* was not only banned in the United States. The right-wing Christian military dictatorship that the United States supported in Greece from 1967–1976 banned Aristophanes and Plato and other classical Greek works, which are the foundation for the free inquiry that has defined Western culture since the Renaissance.

## Let Students Examine Issues

Politically motivated censorship is one thing, but what about telling an experienced teacher that she or he cannot read "Brokeback Mountain" with a class of 18-year-olds? Here we should think like LBJ. Books and ideas are effective against ignorance and intolerance. Most of these students are old enough to volunteer to fight and die in Iraq and Afghanistan. Many are knowledgeable about sex beyond the imaginations of middle-aged parents such as me. And many of them are starving to examine serious issues about life and to have their ideas taken seriously.

Efforts to censor works such as Proulx's short story are sad. On literary or gay and lesbian Web sites, you will read messages like this: "'Brokeback Mountain' is one of the best stories I have ever read. It captures love, beyond borders, and reminds us that we never know how love will come to us. Hope that you recognize it when it does." Our almost-grown children know all about sex. Don't we want them to recognize what love is, too?

### EVALUATING THE AUTHORS' ARGUMENTS:

In this viewpoint Palaima argues that a short story such as "Brokeback Mountain" is valuable reading material for seniors in high school. What do you think Palaima would say about a suggestion—such as that from Warren Throckmorton, author of the previous viewpoint—that parental permission be required before students were allowed to read this story in class?

# Students Need Freedom of Speech

**Sara-Ellen Amster**

*"It was wrong for Oceanside school officials to prevent students from symbolic speech simply because of fear and discomfort with the issue of illegal immigration."*

In the following viewpoint Sara-Ellen Amster argues that students should not be prohibited from displaying patriotic symbols while attending high school. Amster believes that for young people in high school, expressing their ideas is important for the development of their critical skills. She disagrees with the California Oceanside School District's decision to ban the display of all patriotic symbols after concern that displays of American and Mexican flags by various students were contributing to conflict. Learning how to express ideas through student journalism or through peaceful protest or symbols should not be limited to what is comfortable for school administrators, she concludes. Amster is an assistant professor of communication in the School of Media and Communication at National University in Costa Mesa, California. She is the author of *Seeds of Cynicism: The Undermining of Journalistic Education.*

Sara-Ellen Amster, "Teaching Students to Be Citizens," *San Diego Union-Tribune,* April 13, 2006. Reproduced by permission of the author.

I f terrorists threatened to blow up Oceanside High School [in Oceanside, CA] because students wanted to display patriotic symbols there, few of us would have stood for it.

## Student Free Speech Rights

Yet last week [April 3, 2006], school officials "temporarily" prohibited displays of the flag, both U.S. and Mexican, with little outcry from the public. That educators, whose job it is to socialize the next generation for democratic participation, took this absurd stance reveals they cared more about keeping students under control and quiet than teaching them the value of the First Amendment.

It took the officials a week to unapologetically reverse their decision, but the fact that they still believe the ban, "to calm things down," ever made any sense shows continued contempt for democratic principles.

These are difficult times when our cherished freedoms are under attack around the globe by people who want to destroy us. That makes teaching youth about our traditions of freedom, evident in landmark U.S. Supreme Court rulings such as *Tinker v. Des Moines Independent School District* [1969], even more critical. In that case, school officials, similarly frightened of potential disruption, wanted to ban black armbands that young people planned to wear to protest the Vietnam War.

The Court declared that minors do not shed their constitutional right to free expression just because they walk through the schoolhouse gate. School officials feared unrest then and now, but fear of potential disruption should not trump students' First Amendment protections, the Supreme Court found.

*Students in California march in protest using both the American and Mexican flags. The Oceanside, California, school district banned the use of any patriotic symbols because they were afraid it would cause serious conflict among students.*

Immigration and border control are perhaps the most controversial subjects facing young people in Southern California today. An untold number of them either are the children of undocumented immigrants themselves or attend schools with them so that their opinions on this issue matter in a way that requires adult attention. What the students at Oceanside wanted to protest, though, is not really the issue.

## Training for Democracy

As a researcher who studied high school journalism in Southern California for three years (2001–2003), I learned that the unwarranted fears of school officials about youth expressing themselves are actually quite common. Schools did not prove themselves to be places of respect for diversity of thought.

My further experiences as a former journalism teacher and adviser and a journalist, have led me to believe that students have always faced school authorities more worried about parent reaction than building inquisitive citizens and future journalists. The fact is too many of our training programs for democracy—the student press, student government and civics education—are failing, at a historical moment when we can no longer afford to neglect them.

At two of the schools I observed, I did not find much respect for young people's opinions or their rights to free expression as student journalists. The schools and students who agreed to participate are not named in my work.

I know that extending greater freedom to young people may involve school officials having to give up more control over the content of what students express, but schools should not be totalitarian regimes, and educators should inform the students of the rights they enjoy as citizens.

## California Laws

I favor the student press rights we have on the books in California that are supposed to prevent censorship. It's true, building a stronger student press and student government might mean students sometimes turn the spotlight on their schools, but this is hardly negative. To the extent that school officials believe any criticism is a hassle, however, students become timid and self-censoring, rather than gutsy and willing to take on serious questions that also matter to adults.

**FAST FACT**

In April 2006 the American Civil Liberties Union (ACLU) sent a letter to Fallbrook Union High School, in Fallbrook, California, calling the school's discipline of a student for wearing a small American flag a violation of the student's First Amendment rights.

California is lucky. In most other states, the high court has allowed censorship of the student press for any pedagogical reason ever since its 1988 decision in *Hazelwood v. Kuhlmeier*. But the young now are letting us know that what they reap from the lessons of censorship is greater ignorance.

In California, the Education Code provides the extra protection from censorship for student journalists, both at public and private schools, that the Supreme Court did not. But all too often the law is not enforced and relegated to theory. Teachers do not even bother to inform students of their legal rights.

**High school students should be allowed to report controversial issues in their student newspapers without approval of school authorities:**

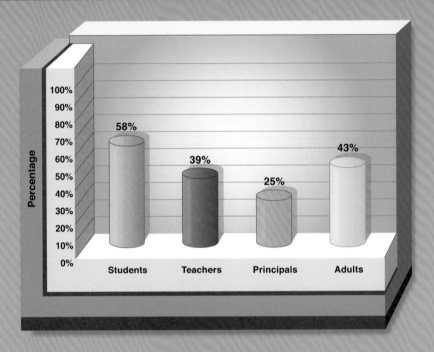

Taken from: John S. and James L. Knight Foundation, "Future of the First Amendment," 2005. www.knightfoundation.org.

## The Importance of Students' Rights

How can schools fulfill their mission of building strong citizens when they do not model any form of democratic principles I know of? More specifically, how can they foster future leaders and writers? Anti-press attitudes are so common that even those who are expected to educate students in journalism end up giving young people a primer in cynicism.

For their voices to count, young people's opinions must first be heard in their homes and schools. No matter whether you think students can be fine journalists, shutting down massive student walkouts was a necessary step to prevent breakdown of order in the schools. Yet it was wrong for Oceanside school officials to prevent students from symbolic speech simply because of fear and discomfort with the issue of illegal immigration. It is one thing to prevent threats and actual disruption; it is quite another to censor ideas or the symbols that represent them.

School officials in Oceanside said the ban on patriotic clothing and symbols was temporary, but peaceful students should never have needed to worry [that] the schools would lift their constitutional rights at any time.

## EVALUATING THE AUTHOR'S ARGUMENTS:

In this viewpoint Amster contends that schools should not be allowed to prevent students from wearing certain kinds of symbolic clothing. Given this, do you think Amster would support a school policy that required all students to wear uniforms? Why or why not?

**Viewpoint**

**6**

# Students Can Rightfully Have Their Speech Limited

*Janesville (WI) Gazette*

> *"Even our constitutional rights to free speech and expression have limits."*

In the following viewpoint the *Janesville Gazette* argues that schools may ban students from wearing certain articles of clothing that could be disruptive; such a ban might include T-shirts of certain bands that are deemed to use offensive lyrics, even if the lyrics are not on the T-shirt. The author discusses a ban enacted by Edgerton High School, in Wisconsin, of T-shirts bearing representations of the Insane Clown Posse, a controversial rap band whose lyrics are seen as promoting violence, misogyny, and homophobia. The *Gazette* contends that the school has an obligation as an employer to avoid a hostile work environment for school employees, in addition to creating a learning environment free from disruption. The *Gazette* believes that such a ban shows students that the First Amendment right is not absolute. The *Janesville Gazette* is a daily newspaper in Janesville, Wisconsin.

"Edgerton Students Getting Lessons in Limits of Rights," *Janesville Gazette,* October 9, 2007. Reproduced by permission.

AS YOU READ, CONSIDER THE FOLLOWING QUESTIONS:
1. Who originally complained about a student's T-shirt at Edgerton High School, according to the author?
2. According to the *Janesville Gazette*, the superintendent of Edgerton High School banned clothing by the Insane Clown Posse because he believes the band promotes what?
3. What is a juggalo, according to the author's description?

*"A scourge is ravaging the American Midwest. It isn't methamphetamines or obesity; the plague is clowns. Followers of the Insane Clown Posse, a group of fat white men from Detroit who rap about the glories of misogyny, homophobia and violence, have small and large towns across the Midwest mired in terror. Several towns have added acolytes of the Insane Clown Posse to a list of currently operating violent gangs."*

—Jeff Merrion, for *The Bygone Bureau*, an independent online publication that focuses on cultural criticism.

Edgerton High School [in Edgerton, Wisconsin,] students are getting a good lesson in how the real world operates.

## School Has Its Own Rules

They live in a democracy, but a school district doesn't operate as a democracy. No place of employment runs as a democracy. In business, you follow the employer's rules, which often include proper attire, or you find another job.

> **FAST FACT**
>
> The U.S. Supreme Court ruled in *Hazelwood v. Kuhlmeier* that school officials have the right to control school-sponsored student publications that are part of school curricula and not designed as public forums of student expression.

Likewise, a school district is an employer. When an Edgerton High staffer complained that the Insane Clown Posse's T-shirts offended her, administrators were justified in investigating. And they were right to ban the clothing. To do otherwise would be to allow a hostile work environment that could lead to a discrimination lawsuit.

# Teen View of Censorship

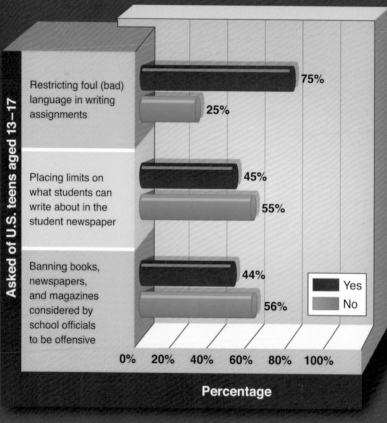

Asked of U.S. teens aged 13–17

**Restricting foul (bad) language in writing assignments**
- 75% (Yes)
- 25% (No)

**Placing limits on what students can write about in the student newspaper**
- 45% (Yes)
- 55% (No)

**Banning books, newspapers, and magazines considered by school officials to be offensive**
- 44% (Yes)
- 56% (No)

Legend: ■ Yes ■ No

Percentage: 0% 20% 40% 60% 80% 100%

Taken from: Gallup poll, "Censorship: Do Teens Bow to School Control?" July 12, 2005.*

*Poll taken April 15–May 22, 2005. www.gallup.com.

## A Ban on Certain Clothing

Late last month, Edgerton administrators sent home senior Matthew D. Richardson, who was wearing an Insane Clown Posse shirt.

Superintendent Norm Fjelstad noted that the band promotes racism and gang violence and hatred of women. He said administrators have the right to restrict clothes that "cross the line where they become disruptive to the school." If administrators didn't have that right, how could a school enact and enforce a dress code?

Fjelstad's decision led to protests and last week's arrests of Richardson and a female student on accusations of threatening the school. Richardson and other students claim it's unfair to ban clothing from one band when others also have offensive lyrics.

But as Janesville Craig Principal Mike Kuehne told the *Gazette*, such incidents must be handled on a case-by-case basis. Often, administrators don't know what an image or logo means until it's brought to their attention. Last year, Craig banned "snowman" shirts made popular by rapper Young Jeezy when they learned the innocent-looking image represents cocaine.

## Free Speech Has Limits

Insane Clown Posse followers are known as juggalos. For *The Bygone Bureau*, Jeff Merrion defines a juggalo as a male adherent to the band's credo of beating women and gays, ingesting large amounts of

*The Edgerton school district banned Insane Clown Posse T-shirts because followers of the band call themselves "juggalos" and adhere to the band's credo of beating women and gays, using psychotropic drugs, and causing general mayhem.*

psychotropic drugs and causing general disorder. It's troubling that young people, especially females, would passionately follow such a band.

Fjelstad said students are showing a natural desire to question authority, but the right way to do that is to take the issue to the school board. He is confident the district's actions are legal because of Supreme Court decisions. "We contacted three attorneys because freedom of speech is a very important issue to us," he told the *Gazette*.

Richardson's mother, former Edgerton City Council member Cindy Richardson, wants the board to resolve the issue or she is prepared to go to court.

This dispute offers lessons in how the world works, and we hope students come away with greater respect for others and the understanding that even our constitutional rights to free speech and expression have limits.

**EVALUATING THE AUTHOR'S ARGUMENTS:**

In this viewpoint the *Janesville Gazette* contends that the clothing ban at Edgerton High School was started by a complaint that the clothing was offensive. Give an example of a piece of attire a student might wear to school that may be offensive to someone but should nonetheless not be banned.

# Chapter 3

# Do New Technologies Need Regulation?

*The use of new technologies, such as Apple's iPod, raise new issues concerning the First Amendment.*

# Some Regulation Is Necessary for New Electronic Media

*"We should have as much ability as possible to assure that electronic commerce is conducted within our laws."*

### David Coursey

In the following viewpoint David Coursey argues that regulation of material on the Internet is consistent with valuing freedom of speech. Coursey argues that some government regulation of speech in media and on the Internet is warranted and does not constitute censorship. Coursey defends the right to express political, artistic, or religious ideas, but he asserts that criminal activity on the Internet, like child pornography, should be prevented whenever possible. Coursey is special correspondent for eWeek.com, where he writes a daily blog and twice-weekly column.

**AS YOU READ, CONSIDER THE FOLLOWING QUESTIONS:**
1. According to Coursey, which European country does not allow television advertising directed at children?
2. What two alternatives, which the author believes would not work, have people suggested for dealing with offshore child pornographers?
3. What solution does the author propose for dealing with Internet material originating from offshore that violates U.S. laws?

David Coursey, "I, Censor?" eWeek.com, September 8, 2005. Reproduced by permission.

There is an idea making the rounds on some blogs that I am in favor of censoring free speech on the Internet. This is based on a misinterpretation of comments I've made to the effect that a national firewall might someday be necessary to protect Americans from Internet crime. While I do not believe commercial speech—cigarette commercials, for example—deserves the same protection as political, artistic or religious expression, I don't think that qualifies me as a censor.

## Free Speech in America

Sweden, for example, does not allow television advertising to be directed at children because they believe it's harmful to them. I think that would be an excellent protection for our children (and parents) as well, but don't think it makes me a censor or Sweden a country that lacks free speech. By the standards of most, perhaps all, European democracies, Americans take free speech to an extreme. I am glad we do, but also accept that with freedom comes responsibility.

It wouldn't bother me if Howard Stern were to be jailed on indecency charges, and I am in favor of keeping the "seven [swear] words" off radio and television. However, if someone wants to stand up in a public square and use those words as part of political, religious or artistic expression, that should be allowed, even encouraged. But, when someone in another country—beyond the reach of American laws—starts serving child pornography to American pedophiles, is it "censorship" to deny them electronic access to their customers? If you think kiddie porn should be protected speech, I really have nothing to say to you.

I am not talking about someone arguing a political position with which I disagree, promoting a religion I'm not a part of, or even posting artwork that I think stinks. I am talking about criminals making money by exploiting children and encouraging pedophiles here in America to continue their illegal activities, but doing this from beyond the reach of our laws. When we find these sites being hosted here in the United States, we have criminal penalties to impose. But what if the site is located in another country? Some people have suggested we deny entry to these criminals when they try to come to the United States or have them arrested where they live and extradited for trial. Both those alternatives are naïve in the extreme and presume the ability to actually find the criminals. Once identified, we'd stop these criminals from entering the United States (why would they want to?) or their local law enforcement would take our complaints seriously and make arrests. If those methods would work, I'd be all for them, but I can't imagine they would be terribly effective.

## The Chinese Government

Yet, when I suggest that it might be worthwhile to have the ability to filter objectionable sites at our electronic borders, I am lumped in with the Chinese, who clearly filter political and religious speech to prop up their Communist dictatorship. Regular readers of my column are well aware that I don't look at the Chinese government's intentions towards the United States as benignly as most of my peers. If

*The ease with which Internet pornography can be downloaded by underage teens has many groups advocating regulating Internet porn.*

my critics were aware of a recent situation, in which I was erroneously led to believe that an American company was providing the Chinese with such filtering software, I think they would better understand my position. It is fair to say I went absolutely ballistic over what I believed was the United States selling censorship tools to the Chinese government. I promptly wrote a column nuking the company involved, but held it because I considered the allegation I was making to be so bizarre. Further investigation allowed the company to demonstrate as conclusively as I considered possible that they wanted nothing more than to give Chinese parents better control over what their children accessed online. The column was appropriately rewritten and took a much more positive slant. I am still watching this company, just in case, though I have no reason to suspect it of any wrongdoing.

**FAST FACT**

According to Internet Watch Foundation, of all known child abuse domains, 54 percent are housed in the United States.

## Our Electronic Borders

I know there are areas where good patriots (of all political stripes) may disagree, but I could never support censoring anyone's right to speak out on political or religious issues. I am concerned, for example, about people posting the directions for making WMD [weapons of mass destruction] materials on the Internet and believe that violent video games and entertainment contribute in measurable ways to a violent society. In these and similar cases, I am not opposed to some sort of regulation, which I understand some would call censorship. I'd rather people just acted responsibly and with concern for others, but if they don't, I think government should be ready to step in.

It's not clear to me that allowing prescription drugs to be advertised directly to patients has improved health care. I think we were better off when such advertising was illegal. But is that really censorship or just good public policy? If the American people, through their elected representatives, decide to regulate online gambling, I believe we should have the option of forcing the issue if offshore Web sites don't want to play by our rules. We don't have to use the option, but it should be available to us. Likewise, we should have as much ability as possible to assure that electronic commerce is conducted within our laws.

There are a number of big sticks at our disposal, but the biggest would be shutting the offending commercial Internet traffic off at our borders. I hope it would never come to this, but there will be criminals out there forcing the issue, and we should respond as we deem necessary. Obviously, I am not someone who believes all speech should be completely unregulated. But most people are that way. We've agreed that yelling "fire" in a crowded theater, threatening to kill someone, or advocating the violent overthrow of the United States all cross the line. There is also a distinction between the free speech that makes democracy possible and that which allows criminals and others to take advantage of us all. I don't think my views make me a censor. But you have the right to call me whatever you like. That's your right—it's free speech.

**EVALUATING THE AUTHOR'S ARGUMENTS:**

In this viewpoint Coursey contends that online material in violation of U.S. laws should be prohibited by the government. Given that pornography sites on the Internet can only ask one's age but not verify it, do you think that Coursey would argue for the elimination of all Internet pornography and not just child pornography?

# Education on Use of New Electronic Media Is Better than Regulation

**Paul K. McMasters**

*"Education is always better than regulation and parents are always better than politicians when it comes to monitoring speech."*

In the following viewpoint Paul K. McMasters claims that demand for regulation of new electronic media is inevitable but should be avoided. McMasters argues that whenever new media communication is created, demands to protect children always end up in a debate about regulation. McMasters contends that past regulation—such as regulation of television and radio—has not worked, leaving him to conclude that regulation of new electronic media should be avoided in favor of allowing parents to regulate the content that children consume. McMasters is the First Amendment ombudsman for the Freedom Forum, a nonpartisan foundation dedicated to free press and free speech.

## AS YOU READ, CONSIDER THE FOLLOWING QUESTIONS:

1. The author claims that every advance in human communication results in what?
2. Complaints to the Federal Communications Commission about indecency recently dropped by how much in one quarter?
3. McMasters believes that efforts to restrict adult expression in order to protect children always end up with what three difficulties?

P lanning on a cell phone, music player, hand-held computer, game player or other portable electronic device for a stocking stuffer this Christmas?

## Sex and Electronic Devices

Whether used as toys or tools, these handy instruments offer a vast array of digital delights and convenience. And for those so inclined and sufficiently savvy, most also are capable of providing adult content: pornography to go.

The adult-entertainment industry has already identified this nifty niche for naughtiness and believes big profits can be made from porn in the pocket. It's well on its way to providing sexy content for the myriad handheld devices that young and old just can't seem to do without.

Adult firms are offering or planning to offer full-length and short adult films for video iPods and other portable devices, sexy video clips for cell phones, trailers of adult films for portable game players and—for video-challenged devices—heavy-breathing "podcasts" are available.

This new direction shouldn't come as a surprise. Every advance in human communication, from the earliest cave drawings to the latest electronic devices, is quickly converted to yet another way to talk about sex. And as much as we deny it or decry it, there always seems to be a large and avid audience for such fare.

## Protecting Children

One online network startup targeting the new video-playing iPod logged half a million downloads of sexy video clips in the first 24 hours after launch. Another site providing videos of nude models recorded a million downloads in a week. A Boston research firm predicts that the porn-in-the-pocket market will reach $200 million a year by 2009.

Unlike their European counterparts, however, U.S. wireless phone carriers that support video devices are not racing to carry racier fare unless and until they can find a way to make sure it reaches only adult customers. The Cellular Telecommunications & Internet Association, a trade group for wireless carriers, is contemplating a rating system—perhaps similar to those in place for movies, television, and video games—to counter demands for regulation.

Such demands are inevitable. When it comes to new technology, as surely as the porn industry is an early exploiter the youngsters are early adapters. That is a dangerous combination in the minds of many parents.

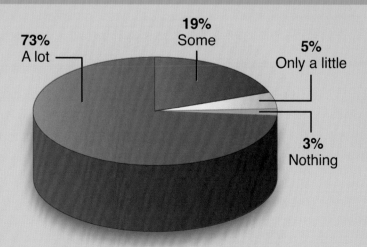

## Parental Monitoring

Overall, how much do you think you know about what your child is doing online, such as whom they are communicating with, what Web sites they are visiting, and what, if anything, they have posted?

73% A lot

19% Some

5% Only a little

3% Nothing

So there will be the anguished lamentations about the end of decency and the ruin of children and angry demands for the government to step in. That is easier demanded than done. The First Amendment rights of content providers as well as adult consumers stand in the way of broad regulations and vague definitions when it comes to restrictions on any form of expression.

In the end, there will be repeated calls from decency advocates for "voluntary" self-regulation by those exploiting this new market with adult content, usually in the form of a ratings system that anti-indecency groups would hope to make part of actual regulation.

## The Decline in Indecency Regulation

One has to look no further than efforts to curb coarseness in the ancient technology of broadcast television and radio to see the limitations—and folly—of that approach.

Right now [December 2005], the Federal Communications Commission [FCC] is struggling to reduce a massive back-up in license renewals for hundreds of television stations across the nation, a back-up created in large part by unresolved complaints of indecency incidents in their broadcasts.

Interestingly, the number of such complaints—many filed in e-mail campaigns by anti-indecency groups—has dropped dramatically. The FCC reported in September [2005] that indecency and obscenity complaints had gone from 157,016 in the first quarter to 6,161 in the second.

For several decades, there has been an uneasy truce in this uneasy area, despite frequent pressure from concerned citizens and occasional posturing by politicians.

FAST FACT

According to a 2009 survey by Harris Interactive and Cox Communications, 80 percent of teens report that their parents know they go online via their cell phone and that they are not given any limits or controls.

The FCC has not pressed the indecency issue too vigorously; the broadcasters have not mounted a forceful First Amendment challenge to indecency regulations in court.

*Many officials argue that parents and educators must be in charge of regulating teens'*
*technology use. It would be virtually impossible for the government to regulate such use,*
*when iPods can download everything from Internet porn to academic cheating tips.*

## Problems with Regulation

That could change, however. Ironically, the FCC's proposed rules on
children's exposure to commercial messages (among other requirements) rather than indecent content finally may bring about that
legal showdown.

Viacom Inc. went to federal court in October [2005] seeking to
overturn new FCC rules extending children's programming requirements in the Children's Television Act of 1990 to the additional
channels made possible by the change from analog to digital signal
transmission. Viacom says it is only seeking review of the new rules,
but industry observers predict that the court action could lay the legal
foundation for a broader challenge to the 1990 law.[1]

Meanwhile, FCC Chairman Kevin J. Martin warns cable and satellite providers that they could face the same regulatory wrath as their
broadcast competitors unless they offer family-friendly options such

1. New digital television guidelines were approved in September 2006, leaving the 1990 law in place.

as "a la carte" subscription to individual channels. In testimony before the Senate Commerce Committee Nov. 29, Martin brushed aside assertions from industry executives that such attempts to create more tools for combating coarseness would result in higher costs and fewer choices for consumers.

That's where these efforts to restrict adult expression in order to protect children usually wind up. The difficulties always arise in the efforts to define decency, legislate taste and police speech.

That's why education is always better than regulation and parents are always better than politicians when it comes to monitoring speech—portable and otherwise.

**EVALUATING THE AUTHORS' ARGUMENTS:**

In this viewpoint McMasters argues that regulation of devices such as iPods, cell phones, and portable game players should be done by parents only. What concern do you think David Coursey, author of the previous viewpoint, might raise about this strategy?

# Obscenity Laws Warrant Censorship of Internet Pornography

**Robert Peters**

> *"The First Amendment does not protect obscene materials."*

In the following viewpoint Robert Peters addresses Barack Obama, who had just been elected president. Peters argues for the enforcement of federal obscenity laws, which he claims prohibit hardcore Internet pornography. Peters claims that many people are victims of this pornography and that, despite what people sometimes think, obscenity is not protected by the U.S. Constitution. Peters claims that the United States has failed at keeping Internet pornography away from juveniles. He concludes that the president ought to make enforcement of obscenity laws a priority, and that such enforcement is backed by the majority of people in the United States. Peters is president of Morality in Media, a nonprofit organization founded in New York City in 1962 to combat obscenity and uphold standards of decency in the media.

**AS YOU READ, CONSIDER THE FOLLOWING QUESTIONS:**
1. What group is among the victims of adult obscenity listed by the author?
2. According to the Supreme Court case *Paris Adult Theater I v. Slaton*, can obscene materials be banned even if juveniles have no access to them?
3. According to Peters, what 1998 law that attempts to enforce federal obscenity laws was invalidated by federal courts?

Dear President-elect Obama:

First, let me congratulate you on Tuesday's [November 4, 2008,] victory. You fought and won a long and difficult campaign against two worthy opponents. But if you now hope to become the President of all Americans, you will have to make policy decisions that citizens who voted for and against you can support.

## Federal Obscenity Laws

I am writing to you again about the need to vigorously enforce federal obscenity laws. I am writing now because planning for a new Administration begins soon after an election. In particular, the individuals you nominate to serve as Attorney General, Director of the FBI and U.S. Attorneys will play crucial roles in the matter of enforcement or non-enforcement of federal obscenity laws.

In the longer term, your nominations for federal judges will also play a crucial role—whether in upholding the laws of the land or in weakening or overturning Constitutional laws necessary for the protection of morality, family life and children. I say "Constitutional laws" because I do not subscribe to the despotic theory that the Constitution is whatever unelected federal judges say it is.

During the campaign, I encouraged both Senator [John] McCain and you to make public your position on enforcement of federal obscenity laws. Both of you chose to remain silent on this issue—as if our nation did not have an already serious and still growing problem with "adult" obscenity, as if the public did not have a right to know or didn't need to know where you stood on this important issue.

## Adult Obscenity

For the record, "adult" obscenity does not depict actual children, but does include hardcore pornographic depictions of sex with persons who look like children, sex with barely legal teens, sex with animals, sex with excrement, sex with family members, sex with multiple partners, sex with prostitutes, sex with she-males, sex with someone else's spouse, and the degradation, rape, and torture of women.

Also for the record, the victims of "adult" obscenity include individuals who participate in hardcore pornography (harms include exposure to sexually transmitted diseases and physical abuse); individuals of all ages who become addicted to hardcore pornography; spouses of individuals who become addicted to hardcore pornography; women who are sexually harassed, sexually assaulted and raped by individuals who are addicted to hardcore pornography; and children and teens who are sexually assaulted by other children and teens who act out what they see in hardcore pornography. Adults who prey on children also use "adult" obscenity to stimulate themselves and to arouse, desensitize and instruct their victims.

## No Protection for Obscenity

Despite what we often read and hear in the mainstream media, the First Amendment does not protect obscene materials. As the Supreme Court stated in a 1973 obscenity case, *Miller v. California*:

*In efforts to enforce the Child Online Protection Act of 1998 FBI agents show some of the technology used to detect child pornography files shared over the Internet.*

This much has been categorically settled by the Court, that obscene material is unprotected by the First Amendment. . . . To equate the free and robust exchange of ideas and political debate with commercial exploitation of obscene material demeans the grand conception of the First Amendment and its high purposes in the historic struggle for freedom. It is a "misuse of the great guarantees of free speech and free press."

In another 1973 obscenity case, *Paris Adult Theater I v. Slaton*, the Supreme Court identified several "legitimate governmental interests" that justify a prohibition on obscene materials *"even if it is feasible to enforce effective safeguards against exposure to juveniles."* [Emphasis supplied.] These interests include protecting the community environment, protecting "public safety," and maintaining "a decent society." The *Paris* Court continued:

> The sum of experience . . . affords an ample basis for legislatures to conclude that a sensitive, key relationship of human existence, central to family life, community welfare, and the development of human personality, can be debased and distorted by crass commercial exploitation of sex.

## Obscenity on the Internet

It is of course no secret that the United States has failed miserably at *"enforcing effective safeguards against exposure to juveniles."* The Internet in particular is awash with hard-core pornographic materials that are available to minors without cost or proof of age; and surveys indicate that large numbers of children have been inadvertently exposed to these materials or have sought them out.

It has failed miserably because federal judges have repeatedly invalidated the Child Online Protection Act of 1998 [COPA],

During the past fifteen years, hardcore pornographic materials have proliferated in the form of videotapes and DVDs sold in sexually oriented and mainstream video stores, films distributed on cable, satellite, and hotel television systems, and still pictures and video disseminated on the Internet. Were the next president [elected in 2008] to do all in his or her constitutional power to ensure that federal obscenity laws are enforced vigorously against commercial distributors of hardcore pornography, would you support or oppose the president in this matter?

**Would you strongly (support/oppose)?**

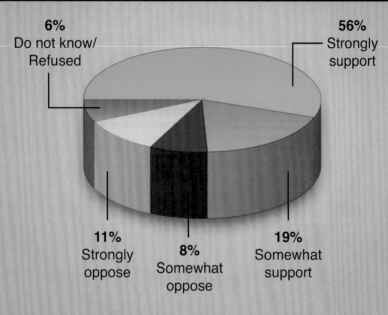

6%
Do not know/
Refused

56%
Strongly
support

11%
Strongly
oppose

8%
Somewhat
oppose

19%
Somewhat
support

Taken from: Harris Interactive/Morality in Media, Inc., April 9, 2008.*

*Poll April 2–6, 2008. www.moralityinmedia.org.

which would require websites that commercially distribute pornography to take reasonable steps to restrict children's access to pornography, and because federal Internet obscenity laws have rarely been enforced since they were enacted in 1996. What the Congressionally created COPA Commission stated in its October 2000 *Final Report* about curbing "adult" obscenity is still largely true:

Law enforcement resources at the state and federal level have focused nearly exclusively on child pornography and child stalking. We believe that an aggressive effort to address illegal, obscene material on the Internet will also address the presence of harmful to minors material.

Citizen organizations involved in the "war against obscenity" have often and rightly criticized the [George W.] Bush Administration for its failure to vigorously enforce federal obscenity laws. But in fairness to the Bush Administration, it has made some progress in the "war against obscenity."

## Support for Enforcement of Obscenity Laws

The choice for you as the next President is either to build on the progress made by your immediate predecessor or to allow the Justice Department to revert to the policy adopted under President Clinton's watch—namely, to give commercial distributors of hardcore pornography a "free ride."

If you choose to be a builder, the large majority of Americans old enough to vote will support you. According to the results of an April 2008 Harris Interactive poll, 75% of Americans 18 years of age and older said they would support the next President were he to do all in his power "to ensure that federal obscenity laws are enforced vigorously against commercial distributors of hardcore pornography." Only 11% said they would "strongly oppose;" another 8% said they would just "somewhat oppose."

> **EVALUATING THE AUTHORS' ARGUMENTS:**
>
> In this viewpoint Peters contends that pornography needs to be prohibited under U.S. obscenity laws. Which of the two previous authors in this chapter, Paul K. McMasters or David Coursey, do you think is more likely to agree with him? Explain your answer.

# Obscenity Laws Should Be Eliminated

## Marjorie Heins

*"Rationality has never reigned in the highly charged sphere of obscenity law."*

In the following viewpoint Marjorie Heins argues that the arrival of the Internet finally shows that obscenity laws need to be abolished. Heins discusses what she takes to be the arbitrary test of obscenity that includes a survey of community standards. Heins contends that with the arrival of the Internet, neither attempting to determine a community standard nor enforcing obscenity laws is reasonable. Marjorie Heins is founder of the Free Expression Policy Project, an organization that provides research and advocacy on free speech, copyright, and media democracy issues. She is the author of *Not in Front of the Children: "Indecency," Censorship, and the Innocence of Youth.*

**AS YOU READ, CONSIDER THE FOLLOWING QUESTIONS:**

1. The first part of the test for obscenity, as described by the author, is that the material in question is patently offensive according to what standards?
2. When did America's first Internet censorship law pass, according to the author?
3. What does Heins suggest as a more effective, as well as constitutionally attractive, answer to concerns about pornography?

Marjorie Heins, "Not in My Backyard," *Index on Censorship*, April 3, 2009. Reproduced by permission of the publisher, www.indexonline.org.

Robert and Carleen Thomas were happily operating the 'Amateur Action Bulletin Board' out of their California home in 1994 when legal hell descended in the form of a federal criminal prosecution for obscenity. The prosecution itself should not have come as a surprise: the US government, like its state and local counterparts, periodically launches campaigns against sexual material that it wants to ban (in this case, the material included online images of bestiality, sadomasochism, and oral sex). What was unusual was the venue the prosecutors chose for the trial: Tennessee, not California. They wanted the conservative community standards of America's 'Bible Belt' to apply to the words and images that the Thomases had posted online.

## The Obscenity Test

US obscenity law is governed by a three-part legal test: whether the material in question is 'patently offensive' according to 'contemporary community standards'; whether it appeals to the 'prurient interest'— again, as determined by community standards; and whether it lacks 'serious literary, artistic, political, or scientific value'. Since the Internet can be accessed anywhere—and the Thomases' bulletin board had been accessed by a government agent in Tennessee—the prosecutors argued the defendants could be subjected to the values and standards of Tennessee, not those of the larger—and decidedly more liberal— cyberspace community.

The courts agreed: the Thomases were convicted by a Tennessee jury and sentenced to prison (37 months for Robert and 30 for Carleen). But the question of what community standards should apply in the global medium of cyberspace continues to haunt that strange and anomalous corner of the law called obscenity. . . . The three-part test for obscenity was created by the Supreme Court in a 1973 case called *Miller v. California.*

## Community Standards

*Miller v. California* was an attempt by the Supreme Court to get out of the business of reviewing every naughty book or film that had been found obscene by a judge or jury; but initially, things did not work out as planned. Just one year later, the Court found itself again in the screening room, overturning a Georgia jury's verdict that the Mike Nichols film *Carnal Knowledge* was obscene. The justices unanimously ruled that the film was not 'patently offensive' according to contemporary community standards.

The Court also now announced (in another case decided the same day) that 'community standards' can be either national or local. That is, 'a juror is entitled to draw on his own knowledge of the views of the average person in the community or vicinage from which he comes', but 'our holding in *Miller* that California could constitutionally proscribe obscenity in terms of a "statewide" standard did not mean that any such precise geographic area is required as a matter of law'. This bit of slippery reasoning seemed to create what lawyers call a 'one-way ratchet': the people of Maine or Mississippi can impose a rigorous local standard on sexual speech because, as Chief Justice [Warren] Burger wrote in *Miller*, they should not have to tolerate the laxity of Las Vegas or New York; but the people of Las Vegas and New York do not necessarily get to benefit from their more robust environment, because the courts do not have to specify any 'precise geographic area' when instructing juries on what 'community standard' means.

And so matters stood, with minor refinements of obscenity law, for the next generation. In 1984, for example, apparently recognising that sex is, after all, a healthy pursuit, the Court announced that 'prurient interest' means only an appeal to 'shameful or morbid' appetites, not 'normal sexual responses'. Local juries would now get to decide what is healthy or unhealthy in the bedroom.

## The Internet

Then the Internet arrived, and with it a full-fledged revival of the community standards dilemma. Although the courts in Robert and

Carleen Thomas' case managed to skirt the constitutional concerns raised by local community standards when applied to the Internet, because the Thomases had specific knowledge that a Tennesseean had joined their group, a clash between small-town morality and global communication seemed inevitable. Could puritanical localities really impose their sexual standards on all of cyberspace?

Initially, the Supreme Court seemed decidedly hostile to such an outcome. America's first Internet censorship law, passed in 1996, criminalised any sexual speech online if it is available to minors and is 'indecent'—that is, 'patently offensive as measured by contemporary community standards'. Striking down the law in a 1997 case called *Reno v. ACLU*, the Supreme Court noted among its many faults that 'the "community standards" criterion as applied to the Internet means that any communication available to a nationwide audience will be judged by the standards of the community most likely to be offended by the message'.

## The Child Online Protection Act

Congress quickly passed another, narrower law restricting online speech, but it did not address the problem of community standards. The 'Child Online Protection Act' or 'COPA', replaced the broad 'indecency' test with a less sweeping legal standard called 'harmful to minors' (also sometimes called 'Miller Lite', because it incorporates all three prongs of the *Miller v. California* definition of obscenity—prurience, patent offensiveness, and lack of serious value—and then applies them to adolescents and children). The American Civil Liberties Union soon filed a constitutional challenge to COPA on behalf of online publishers ranging from *Philadelphia Gay News* to Condomania.

Because the Miller Lite test, like Miller itself, turns on community standards, the question was now squarely presented: does the First Amendment permit a local 'contemporary community standard' for obscenity in cyberspace? A federal court of appeals, confronted with COPA, said 'no', because such a standard would force Internet speakers to self-censor valuable expression for fear of prosecution in the most conservative communities.

The government appealed to the Supreme Court, which now backed away from its initial recognition in *Reno v. ACLU* of the con-

*The ACLU's Ann Beeson speaks at a news conference outside the Supreme Court on March 2, 2004, about the ACLU's suit on behalf of online entrepreneurs that the Child Online Protection Act violates the First Amendment.*

stitutional perils of allowing local standards to dictate speech online. Justice Clarence Thomas, writing for the Court, produced more of the slippery reasoning that has characterised obscenity law from the outset: the variability of community standards is not enough in itself to invalidate COPA, he said, because COPA has the additional limitations of prurient appeal and lack of serious value for minors. (The case went back to the lower courts, which invalidated COPA on other grounds. In January 2009, the Act was finally interred [buried] when the Supreme Court denied further review.)

## An American Standard

When the right case comes along—which will not necessarily be soon—the justices of the US Supreme Court will presumably decide that applying local community standards is not really viable for the

Internet. That is, 'the people of Maine or Mississippi' cannot expect to dictate what is morally permissible in a global medium. Indeed, in their first encounter with COPA, five justices joined in concurring opinions arguing that we need to return to a national standard.

An American national standard, of course, does not take account of the differing cultures that share the web, and imposing American sexual morality on the rest of the world is no more palatable than is censoring the entire Internet to please the Chinese government or, for that matter, purging the entire Internet of racist hate speech because it is illegal in Germany and France. Should sexual material from outside the US, therefore, be blocked to American viewers, if it is thought prurient and patently offensive by American 'community standards', in the same way that Internet access providers now block material from Chinese, French or other viewers in order to comply with these nations' laws? The prospect is daunting, for most countries have laws against obscenity, each with its own peculiar definitions.

## The End of Obscenity Laws

The rational answer is that obscenity laws in the US should be eliminated, as Justices [William O.] Douglas and [Hugo] Black argued a half-century ago, because they have no justification under the First Amendment: moral offence is not the same as palpable harm, and societal fears about minors' exposure to pornography have never been backed up by credible evidence that such exposure in itself distorts their sexual development. Good sex education, for young and old (and middle-aged), is a more effective and constitutionally palatable answer to concerns about pornography.

But rationality has never reigned in the highly charged sphere of obscenity law, and things are not likely to change, at least not judicially, now that the Internet offers instantaneous access to a universe of words and images, some of them admittedly horrible. (Homicidal racism is an example.) One possible future scenario is that the technology of the Internet will ultimately render obscenity laws ineffective and obsolete.

Another, however, is that those who control online content—at this point, primarily corporate Internet access providers, portals, and search engines—will impose a private 'community standard' of their own. That would be an outcome that even the people of Maine and Mississippi might find unfortunate.

# Library Internet Filters Are Necessary

**Arlene Sawicki**

*"An adult library patron has no individual entitlement to access obscene materials on public access Internet."*

In the following viewpoint Arlene Sawicki argues that public libraries need to install software filters to prevent both adults and children from viewing obscene materials on the Internet. Sawicki argues that just as public libraries do not stock print pornography, libraries ought not make pornography on the Internet available to patrons. Sawicki objects to the viewing of pornographic materials in libraries both because she does not believe the public should pay for such activities and also because she believes it could create a hostile work environment for library employees. Sawicki is a long-time Catholic lay advocate for pro-life and pro-family issues and cofounder of Vote Life America.

AS YOU READ, CONSIDER THE FOLLOWING QUESTIONS:
1. According to Sawicki, what group has taken control of how community libraries are run?
2. The library does not function as what, according to the author?
3. The author claims that filtering the Internet in libraries is not censorship but the application of what two things?

After several years of public debate, the controversy over whether to filter taxpayer-funded computers in our public libraries rumbles on. While some local libraries in our communities have installed filtering safeguards [mostly on children's computers] many Library Boards refuse to even consider filters, claiming that doing so violates the First Amendment free access to all information or that filtering software has not yet reached perfection.

## A Concern About Libraries

Our communities should find this apparent reluctance unacceptable. They should find that federal funding will be jeopardized by their libraries' unwillingness to cooperate with federal guidelines for the Children's Internet Protection Act [2000] in filtering obscenity out of both adult and children's terminals.

It is my understanding that parents in some communities are not even allowed to ask questions about filtering safeguards from their Library Boards. This parental restriction would be consistent with another strange "privacy" policy recommended by the American Library Association that parents are not permitted entry into their children's library records. The question begs asking, just how "family friendly" are our area public libraries?

We all value our taxpayer funded community libraries and treasure the variety of information, programs and services it offers. Libraries bring the world to our doorstep and our librarians are instrumental in aiding our thirst for knowledge. But who is really in control of library policies?

## The American Library Association

Whether we are aware of it or not, the American Library Association [ALA], which is a private organization of librarians with no legal or governmental authority, has systematically taken control of how our community libraries are run. They set the agenda, they dictate the policies. A visit to their web site will inform you that the ALA, which is strongly influenced by the ACLU [American Civil Liberties Union], is very much concerned about First Amendment rights, Civil Liberties, Freedom to Read and Privacy policies—as they interpret them.

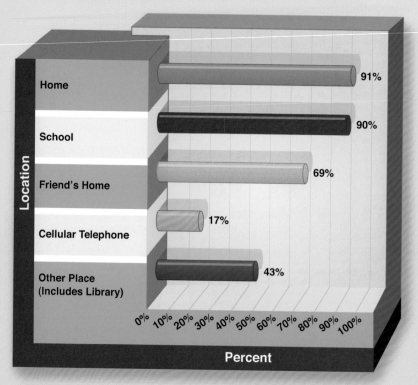

**Location(s) Where Youth Spent Time on the Internet, 2005**

- Home — 91%
- School — 90%
- Friend's Home — 69%
- Cellular Telephone — 17%
- Other Place (Includes Library) — 43%

Location

Percent

Taken from: Janis Wolak, Kimberly Mitchell, David Finkelhor of the Crimes Against Children Research Center, "Online Victimization of Youth: Five Years Later," National Center for Missing and Exploited Children, 2006.

The ALA has come under heated criticism the last few years as it adamantly opposes the filtering of library computers, citing First Amendment and freedom of access rights. The ALA even challenged the Children's Internet Protection Act on constitutional grounds and lost its case when the Supreme Court, in *United States v. the American Library Association* [2003] ruled that filtering computers does not violate their patron's constitutional rights.

The ALA presents itself as a champion for "civil rights," however in challenging a Federal law that would protect the safety of children using the Internet, many judged this radical move as an irresponsible attempt at civil disobedience and a violation of "citizen's rights."

The ALA's web site once contained a link to a sexually-explicit educational resource aimed at children entitled "Go Ask Alice," which came under public scrutiny and fire by talk-show host Dr. Laura Schlessinger. The ALA had also offered children advice on how to work around or undo filtering devices that their parents have installed on home computers. These actions speak volumes regarding this organization's liberal social agenda, which clearly undermines parental authority.

## Obscenity in Libraries

The ALA's misguided idea that the First Amendment protects all forms of speech is patently false. State and Federal Obscenity laws are in place that restrict the distribution of illegal, obscene matter [as ruled by the Supreme Court in *Miller v. California,* 1973]. Transmitting obscenity and child pornography, whether via the Internet or other means, is illegal under federal law for both adults and juveniles.

In October 2003, President [George W.] Bush increased federal efforts to promote online safety against the exploitation of children using the Internet. He expressed his commitment by stating, "Anyone who targets a child for harm will be a primary target of law enforcement. Anyone who takes the life or innocence of a child, will be punished to the full extent of the law." Should the ALA and our libraries hold themselves above the law?

Let us consider the following points: There is nothing written in the First Amendment that mandates libraries to provide obscene or illegal materials to its patrons—adults or children—at the taxpayer's expense. The library does not function as an Internet Service Provider. Its Internet privileges should not be regarded as an "electronic sanctuary" for illegal activity. The library does not collect pornography in print; that selective policy should be extended to pornography by Internet. It should not facilitate and aid the porn industry in distributing and

FAST FACT

According to *Internet Filter Review,* 4.2 million pornographic Web sites were on the Internet as of 2009, which is 12 percent of all Web sites.

*The author argues because public libraries do not stock pornography on their shelves they should not make pornography available on the Internet.*

profiting from illegal trafficking—a predicate offense under R.I.C.O. [Racketeer Influenced and Corrupt Organizations Act].

The protection of children from exposure to lewd and harmful materials should be a matter of compelling and prioritized community interest. The Board of Directors has a fiduciary duty to be open to community involvement and input. An adult library patron has no individual entitlement to access obscene materials on public access Internet. Library patrons and employees have the right to be protected from a sexually hostile work environment, which would not be the case if adults are allowed to arouse themselves by viewing sexually-explicit materials.

In short, the public dissemination of illegal obscene material or child pornography is inconsistent with the Library's prime mission and respect for community standards.

## Filtering Is Not Censorship

My recommendation to all taxpayer-funded public Library Boards is to uphold the highest standards of safety and protection to the community by installing the best computer filtering software available today—on both adult and children's computers. Filtering is not "censorship," it is the application of common sense and decency—despite what the American Library Association would compel their members to do.

If library patrons are seeking pornographic materials, they have the "freedom to read" in the "privacy" of their own homes and on their own dime.

**EVALUATING THE AUTHOR'S ARGUMENTS:**

In this viewpoint, Sawicki argues that filtering Internet pornography should not be a problem since public libraries do not stock print pornography. In what way is Internet pornography different from print pornography in terms of the library providing access to it?

# Library Internet Filters Threaten Freedom

## Marjorie Heins, Christina Cho, and Ariel Feldman

*"The widespread use of filters presents a serious threat to our most fundamental free expression values."*

In the following viewpoint, Marjorie Heins, Christina Cho, and Ariel Feldman argue that Internet filters are terribly imprecise, blocking many more Web sites than necessary in the attempt to block obscenity. The authors give examples of many obscenity-free Web sites that are blocked by filtering software. They conclude that attempting to filter out obscenity from libraries in this manner ends up censoring a wide variety of legitimate information, violating free expression values. Heins is founder of the Free Expression Policy Project; Cho is coordinator of advising for the College of Science, University of Nevada at Reno; Feldman is a PhD student in the Computer Science Department and the Center for Information Technology Policy at Princeton University. The Brennan Center for Justice at New York University School of Law is a nonpartisan public policy and law institute that focuses on fundamental issues of democracy and justice.

Marjorie Heins, Christina Cho, and Ariel Feldman, *Internet Filters: A Public Policy Report,* New York, NY: Brennan Center for Justice, 2006. Reproduced by permission.

**AS YOU READ, CONSIDER THE FOLLOWING QUESTIONS:**

1. The authors state that some policy makers believe that filtering software inaccuracies are an acceptable cost for what goal?
2. According to the authors, a member of the House of Representatives had his Web site blocked by several blocking software programs because of what?
3. What law did the U.S. Supreme Court uphold in 2003 despite evidence of inaccurate filtering products, according to the authors?

E very new technology brings with it both excitement and anxiety. No sooner was the Internet upon us in the 1990s than anxiety arose over the ease of accessing pornography and other controversial content. In response, entrepreneurs soon developed filtering products. By the end of the decade, a new industry had emerged to create and market Internet filters.

## The Problem with Filters

These filters were highly imprecise. The problem was intrinsic to filtering technology. The sheer size of the Internet meant that identifying potentially offensive content had to be done mechanically, by matching "key" words and phrases; hence, the blocking of Web sites for "Middle*sex* County," "*Beaver* College," and "*breast* cancer"— just three of the better-known among thousands of examples of overly broad filtering. Internet filters were crude and error-prone because they categorized expression without regard to its context, meaning, and value.

> **FAST FACT**
>
> Schools and libraries subject to the Children's Internet Protection Act (CIPA) are required to have an Internet safety policy that blocks access on computers accessed by minors to pictures that are (a) obscene, (b) child pornography, or (c) harmful to minors.

Some policymakers argued that these inaccuracies were an acceptable cost of keeping the Internet safe, especially for kids. Others— including many librarians, educators, and civil libertarians—argued that the cost was too high. To help inform this policy debate, the Free Expression Policy Project (FEPP) published a report in the fall of 2001 summarizing the results of more than 70 empirical studies on the performance of Internet filters. These studies ranged from anecdotal accounts of blocked sites to extensive research applying social-science methods.

## Examples of Inaccuracies

Nearly every study revealed substantial overblocking. That is, even taking into account that filter manufacturers use broad and vague blocking categories—for example, "violence," "tasteless/gross," or "lifestyle"—their products arbitrarily and irrationally blocked many Web pages that had no relation to the disapproved content categories. For example:

- Net Nanny, SurfWatch, CYBERsitter, and Bess blocked House Majority Leader Richard "Dick" Armey's official Web site upon detecting the word "dick."
- SmartFilter blocked the Declaration of Independence, Shakespeare's complete plays, *Moby Dick*, and *Marijuana: Facts for Teens*, a brochure published by the National Institute on Drug Abuse.
- SurfWatch blocked the human rights site Algeria Watch and the University of Kansas's Archie R. Dykes Medical Library (upon detecting the word "dykes").
- CYBERsitter blocked a news item on the Amnesty International site after detecting the phrase "least 21." (The offending sentence described "at least 21" people killed or wounded in Indonesia.)
- X-Stop blocked Carnegie Mellon University's Banned Books page, the "Let's Have an Affair" catering company, and, through its "foul word" function, searches for *Bastard Out of Carolina* and "The Owl and the Pussy Cat."

## Filters Are Still Flawed

Despite such consistently irrational results, the Internet filtering business continued to grow. Schools and offices installed filters on their computers, and public libraries came under pressure to do so. In December 2000, President Bill Clinton signed the "Children's

*Internet users surf the Internet without filters at the Philadelphia Public Library. Opponents of filters say the filters block too much content that is not obscene or offensive.*

Internet Protection Act," mandating filters in all schools and libraries that receive federal aid for Internet connections. The Supreme Court upheld this law in 2003 despite extensive evidence that filtering products block tens of thousands of valuable, inoffensive Web pages.

In 2004, FEPP, now part of the Brennan Center for Justice at N.Y.U. School of Law, decided to update the *Internet Filters* report—a project that continued through early 2006. We found several large studies published during or after 2001, in addition to new, smaller-scale tests of filtering products. Studies by the U.S. Department of Justice, the Kaiser Family Foundation, and others found that despite improved technology and effectiveness in blocking some pornographic content, filters are still seriously flawed. They continue to deprive their users of many thousands of valuable Web pages, on subjects ranging from war and genocide to safer sex and public health. Among the hundreds of examples:

- WebSENSE blocked "Keep Nacogdoches Beautiful," a Texas cleanup project, under the category of "sex," and The Shoah Project, a Holocaust remembrance page, under the category of "racism/hate."
- Bess blocked all Google and AltaVista image searches as "pornography."

- Google's SafeSearch blocked congress.gov and shuttle.nasa.gov; a chemistry class at Middlebury College; Vietnam War materials at U.C.-Berkeley; and news articles from the *New York Times* and *Washington Post*.

The conclusion of the revised and updated *Internet Filters: A Public Policy Report* is that the widespread use of filters presents a serious threat to our most fundamental free expression values. There are much more effective ways to address concerns about offensive Internet content. Filters provide a false sense of security, while blocking large amounts of important information in an often irrational or biased way. Although some may say that the debate is over and that filters are now a fact of life, it is never too late to rethink bad policy choices.

## EVALUATING THE AUTHORS' ARGUMENTS:

In this viewpoint, Heins, Cho, and Feldman argue that Internet filters should not be used because of the large number of Web sites the software inaccurately blocks. If the software could be improved so that almost no sites were inaccurately blocked, how do you think these authors would feel about using it? Explain your answer.

# Facts About Censorship

Editor's note: These facts can be used in reports or papers to reinforce or add credibility when making important points or claims.

## The Meaning of Censorship
- The Latin word *censere* means to give one's opinion or to assess.
- The origin of the term *censor* in English can be traced to the office of censor established in Rome in 443 B.C., responsible for maintaining the census of citizens, supervising manners and morals, and overseeing government finance.
- Censorship is the action of suppressing speech or communicative actions, images, or other forms of information either through law or other channels in a way that prevents these forms of communication from being accessed.

## Types of Censorship and Notable Examples
- *Books*: Mark Twain's *The Adventures of Huckleberry Finn* was first banned in 1885 in the Concord Public Library in Massachusetts.
- *Music*: In 1956 ABC radio refused to play Billie Holiday's song "Love for Sale" because the lyrics are about prostitution.
- *Visual Art*: A retrospective of photographer Robert Mapplethorpe's work, *Robert Mapplethorpe: The Perfect Moment,* was cancelled in 1989 by the Corcoran Gallery of Art in Washington, D.C., after members of Congress complained: The show had been organized by an institute receiving federal National Endowment for the Arts (NEA) money, and some members of Congress claimed that Mapplethorpe's images were obscene.
- *Political Speech*: In 1948 the U.S. House of Representatives Un-American Activities Committee held hearings into alleged Communist influence in the Hollywood film industry, convicting ten writers and directors of contempt for refusing to answer questions about their political beliefs. These convictions resulted in one-year prison sentences for each. Following this, hundreds of Hollywood screenwriters, actors, directors, and other film professionals were

blacklisted, or denied employment, during the 1950s due to their suspected political beliefs.

## Justifications Given for Censorship
- **political harm:** When material is censored to prevent political upheaval.
- **moral harm:** When material is censored due to a concern about moral influence on consumers.
- **religious harm:** When material is censored because it offends a particular religious group.
- **military harm:** When material is censored due to an asserted need to keep military intelligence secret from a perceived enemy.

## The Committee to Protect Journalists' "10 Most Censored Countries," 2006
1. North Korea
2. Burma
3. Turkmenistan
4. Equatorial Guinea
5. Libya
6. Eritrea
7. Cuba
8. Uzbekistan
9. Syria
10. Belarus

# Organizations to Contact

The editors have compiled the following list of organizations concerned with the issues debated in this book. The descriptions are derived from materials provided by the organizations. All have publications or information available for interested readers. The list was compiled on the date of publication of the present volume; the information provided here may change. Be aware that many organizations take several weeks or longer to respond to inquiries, so allow as much time as possible for the receipt of requested materials.

**American Civil Liberties Union (ACLU)**
125 Broad St., 18th Floor
New York, NY 10004
(212) 549-2500
e-mail: infoaclu@aclu.org
Web site: www.aclu.org

The American Civil Liberties Union is a national organization that works to defend Americans' civil rights as guaranteed in the U.S. Constitution. The ACLU works in courts, legislatures, and communities to defend First Amendment rights, the right to equal protection, the right to due process, and the right to privacy. The ACLU publishes the semiannual newsletter *Civil Liberties Alert* as well as other publications, including *Reclaiming Our Rights: Declaration of First Amendment Rights and Grievances.*

**American Library Association (ALA)**
50 E. Huron St.
Chicago, IL 60611
(800) 545-2433
fax: (312) 440-9374
e-mail: ala@ala.org
Web site: www.ala.org

The ALA is the nation's primary professional organization for librarians. The ALA focuses on the development, promotion, and improvement of library services and librarianship in order to enhance learning and ensure access to information. The ALA publishes the online *Newsletter on Intellectual Freedom*, which reports attempts to remove materials from school and public library shelves across the country.

**Enough Is Enough (EIE)**
746 Walker Rd., Ste. 116
Great Falls, VA 22066
(888) 744-0004
fax: (571) 333-5685
Web site: www.enough.org

EIE is a nonpartisan organization that works to make the Internet safer for children and families, free from sexual predators and the intrusion of unwanted sexual material. EIE attempts to raise public awareness about pornography and sexual predation online, encourage the technology industry to implement family-friendly solutions, and promote legal solutions calling for enforcement of existing laws and enactment of new laws to protect children using the Internet. EIE created the Internet Safety 101: Empowering Parents program and the Protect Kids Web site available at www .protectkids.com.

**Family Research Council (FRC)**
801 G St. NW
Washington, DC 20001
(202) 393-2100
fax: (202) 393-2134
Web site: www.frc.org

FRC is an organization dedicated to the promotion of marriage and family and the sanctity of human life in national policy. FRC's team of policy experts reviews data and analyzes proposals that impact family law and policy in Congress and the executive branch. In addition to filing amicus briefs in relevant court cases, FRC publishes several brochures and other publications, including *Internet Guide for Parents* and "Enforcing Broadcast Decency."

**Freedom Forum**
555 Pennsylvania Ave. NW
Washington, DC 20001
(202) 292-6100
e-mail: news@freedomforum.org
Web site: www.freedomforum.org

The Freedom Forum is a nonpartisan foundation dedicated to free press, free speech, and free spirit. The forum's First Amendment Center (www.firstamendmentcenter.org) works to preserve and protect First Amendment freedoms through information and education. It publishes the annual report *State of the First Amendment* as well as numerous publications related to censorship, including "Banned and Challenged Books: A Selected Timeline."

**Index on Censorship**
Free Word Centre, 60 Farringdon Rd.
London, EC1R 3GA, United Kingdom
44 (0) 20 7324 2522
e-mail: enquiries@indexoncensorship.org
Web site: www.indexoncensorship.org

Index on Censorship is Britain's leading organization promoting freedom of expression. Its Web site provides current news and information on free expression from around the world. The organization publishes the magazine *Index on Censorship.*

**Morality in Media (MIM)**
475 Riverside Dr., Ste. 239
New York, NY 10115
(212) 870-3222
fax: (212) 870-2765
e-mail: mim@moralityinmedia.org
Web site: www.moralityinmedia.org

MIM is a national nonprofit organization established to combat obscenity and uphold decency standards in the media. MIM works to inform the public about the harms of pornography and how the law can be used to protect their communities. MIM publishes the quarterly newsletter *Morality in Media* as well as several articles on obscenity and indecency, including "Children Are Only a Few Clicks Away from Being Exposed to Pornography on MySpace.com."

## National Coalition Against Censorship (NCAC)
275 Seventh Ave., Ste. 1504
New York, NY 10001
(212) 807-6222
fax: (212) 807-6245
e-mail: ncac@ncac.org
Web site: www.ncac.org

NCAC is an alliance of fifty-two participating organizations dedicated to protecting free expression and access to information. It has many projects dedicated to educating the public and protecting free expression, including the Free Expression Policy Project, the Kids' Right to Read Project, the Knowledge Project: Censorship and Science, and the Youth Free Expression Network. Among its publications are "Abstinence-Only Education" and *The First Amendment in Schools.*

## National Coalition for the Protection of Children & Families
800 Compton Rd., Ste. 9224
Cincinnati, OH 45231
(513) 521-6227
fax: (513) 521-6337
Web site: www.nationalcoalition.org

The National Coalition for the Protection of Children & Families works to encourage people to embrace, preserve, and advance the truth of biblical sexuality. The coalition focuses on educating Christians about sexual ethics, encouraging Christians to live sexually pure lives, engaging Christians in public policy relative to sexual ethics, and embracing those harmed by pornography. It publishes several booklets addressing the issue of raising kids in a sexualized culture of new technology, including *Sex and Cell Phones: Protect Your Children.*

## Parents Television Council (PTC)
707 Wilshire Blvd., #2075
Los Angeles, CA 90017
(800) 882-6868

fax: (213) 403-1301

e-mail: editor@parentstv.org

Web site: www.parentstv.org

The PTC is an advocacy organization whose primary mission is to promote responsibility and decency in the entertainment industry. The PTC seeks to discourage graphic sexual themes, depictions of gratuitous violence, and profane language in broadcast television through citizen action. Among the PTC's special reports are *Top 10 Best and Worst Advertisers* and *The Alarming Family Hour—No Place for Children*.

**People for the American Way (PFAW)**

2000 M St. NW, Ste. 400

Washington, DC 20036

(202) 467-4999

Web site: www.pfaw.org

PFAW is an organization that fights for progressive values: equal rights, freedom of speech, religious liberty, and equal justice under the law for every American. PFAW works to build and nurture communities of support for their values and to equip those communities to promote progressive policies, elect progressive candidates, and hold public officials accountable. Among its publications on the topic of freedom of speech is the report *Back to School with the Religious Right*.

# For Further Reading

## Books

Beattie, Scott. *Community, Space, and Online Censorship*. Surrey, UK: Ashgate, 2009. Compares Australian, American, and British Internet regulatory systems, exploring the uncontrollable nature of the Internet.

Blecha, Peter. *Taboo Tunes: A History of Banned Books and Censored Songs*. Milwaukee, WI: Backbeat, 2004. Recounts the travails of musicians who have dared to air unacceptable topics, highlighting the work of hundreds of controversial musicians.

Caso, Frank. *Censorship*. New York: Facts On File, 2008. Examines the history and current practices of censorship in five countries—the United States, Russia, China, Zimbabwe, and Egypt—and discusses key counterstrategies.

Couvares, Francis G., ed. *Movie Censorship and American Culture*. Amherst: University of Massachusetts Press, 2006. Eleven essays examine nearly a century of struggle over cinematic representations of sex, crime, violence, religion, race, and ethnicity, revealing that the effort to regulate the screen has reflected deep social and cultural schisms.

Dadge, David. *Silenced: International Journalists Expose Media Censorship*. Amherst, NY: Prometheus, 2005. Recounts stories by journalists worldwide who were threatened with censorship, but chose to report and face the consequences.

Feldman, Stephen M. *Free Expression and Democracy in America: A History*. Chicago: University of Chicago Press, 2008. Traces two rival traditions in American culture—suppression of speech and dissent as a form of speech—to provide an overview of the law, history, and politics of individual rights in the United States.

Green, Jonathan. *Encyclopedia of Censorship*. Revised by Nicholas J. Karolides. New York: Facts On File, 2005. Presents a full range of information about the history and evolution of censorship, and its role in society today.

Heins, Marjorie. *Not in Front of the Children: "Indecency," Censorship, and the Innocence of Youth*. Piscataway, NJ: Rutgers University Press,

2007. Explores the history of indecency laws and other restrictions aimed at protecting youth, with examples from around the globe.

Jennings, Brian, and Sean Hannity. *Censorship: The Threat to Silence Talk Radio.* New York: Threshold, 2009. Argues that a battle for the airwaves underway in America could sharply curtail or silence altogether the freedom of expression that distinguishes the United States from a dictatorship.

Karolides, Nicholas J., Margaret Bald, and Dawn B. Sova. *120 Banned Books: Censorship Histories of World Literature.* New York: Checkmark, 2005. Traces the censorship histories of 120 works from around the world, providing a summary of each work, its censorship history, and suggestions for further reading.

O'Leary, Brad. *Shut Up, America! The End of Free Speech.* Los Angeles: WND, 2009. Contends that a frightening movement is gaining ground in America that would eviscerate the First Amendment, increasing censorship.

Petley, Julian. *Censorship: A Beginner's Guide.* Oxford, UK: Oneworld, 2009. Offers a history of the phenomenon of censorship from the execution of Socrates to the latest in Internet filtering, providing an impassioned manifesto for freedom of speech.

Ringmar, Erik A. *A Blogger's Manifesto: Free Speech and Censorship in the Age of the Internet.* New York: Anthem, 2007. Claims that there was never true freedom of speech until the age of the Internet and calls for principles of free speech to be embraced within this medium.

Silverman, David S. *You Can't Air That: Four Cases of Controversy and Censorship in American Television Programming.* Syracuse, NY: Syracuse University Press, 2007. Assesses four controversial television programs from the perspective of media history, analyzing the role of censorship and the impact on broadcast television.

## Periodicals

Ahmed, Rizwan. "Battling the Censor," *New Statesman,* August 28, 2006.

Alexander, Gerard. "Illiberal Europe," *Weekly Standard,* April 10, 2006.

Alterman, Eric. "Fool Me Once . . .," *Nation,* January 23, 2006.

Andersen, Kurt. "What the [bleep]?! The FCC's Scary New Censorship Crusade Raises the Question: Should the Government Be in the Decency Business at All Anymore?" *New York,* June 5, 2006.

August, Oliver. "Staring Down the Censors," *Wired*, November 2007.

Bhattacharjee, Yudhijit. "Scientific Openness: Should Academics Self-Censor Their Findings on Terrorism?" *Science*, May 19, 2006.

Blankley, Tony. "Yes, We Need Censorship," *Washington Times*, February 12, 2009.

Bradbury, Kelsey. "Authors of Teen Novels Defend Their Right to Tackle Tough Subjects," *Buffalo News*, September 27, 2006.

Buckley, William F., Jr. "The Search for Decency," *National Review*, May 22, 2006.

Cavanaugh, Tim. "Cartoons Make Cowards of Us All," *Reason*, May 2006.

*Christian Science Monitor.* "From China to Denmark, Media Lessons," February 7, 2006.

Collins, Ronald K.L., and David L. Hudson Jr. "Laws Against Funeral Protests Strike at the First Amendment," *Legal Intelligencer*, April 21, 2006.

Cooke, Dominic. "An Insidious Form of Censorship: Dominic Cooke on Why We Must Guard Against a Self-Perpetuating Climate of Fear and Timidity," *Spectator*, October 11, 2008.

Cooper, Horace. "Freedom to Speak: One Community's 'Responsiveness' Is Another's Censorship," *Washington Times*, December 5, 2008.

*Dallas Morning News.* "Libraries Not for Porn: Dallas Has Obligation to Install Interact Filters," January 19, 2008.

Dennies, Joe. "Civics 101: Censoring Students Robs Democracy," *Atlanta Journal-Constitution*, October 26, 2007.

Downey, Maureen. "Student Journalists . . . Need to Learn First Amendment Is Shield for Free Speech, Not Cocoon for Ignorance, Vulgarity," *Atlanta Journal-Constitution*, October 3, 2007.

Dumenco, Simon. "The FCC Thinks You Would Look Totally Hot in a Diaper," *Advertising Age*, June 5, 2006.

Floyer, Sally. "Brought to Book: Halt the Censorship: Literature Is a Great Way for Children to Be Able to Discuss Issues That Trouble and Concern Them," *Bookseller*, September 19, 2008.

Gartenstein-Ross, Daveed. "Legislating Religious Correctness," *Daily Standard*, October 27, 2005.

*Gazette* (Colorado Springs, CO). "Shushing Christians: Of Hypocrites and Academic Freedom," February 6, 2008.

Goldberg, Jonah. "The Twinkie Approach," *National Review Online*, March 1, 2007.

Guider, Elizabeth. "Showbiz in Shackles," *Variety*, March 13, 2006.

Hogge, Becky. "A Year of Browsers—and Censors," *New Statesman*, December 22, 2008.

*International Herald Tribune*. "Joe Lieberman, Would-Be Censor," May 26, 2008.

Just, Richard. "Censorship Hurts Budding Journalists, and Democracy," *Capital Times* (Madison, WI), January 30, 2008.

Koppelman, Andrew. "Reading Lolita at Guantanamo," *Dissent*, Spring 2006.

Kushner, Adam B. "Repression 2.0," *Newsweek International*, April 14, 2008.

Lazar, Rachel. "Censor This! Notice Something Missing?" *New Moon*, January/February 2006.

Lo Monte, Frank D. "Student Journalism Confronts a New Generation of Legal Challenges," *Human Rights*, Summer 2008.

*Maclean's*. "A Small Victory for Free Speech," October 27, 2008.

Meyers, Michael. "Don't Give In to the Censors," *Record* (Bergen County, NJ), April 12, 2007.

Mulshine, Paul. "Will the Censors Please Shut Up? Attacking Ann Coulter, the P.C. Police Show They Don't Understand Religion or Freedom," *Star-Ledger* (Newark, NJ), October 18, 2007.

Otanez, Andrea. "Giving Student Journalists Ownership of Their Papers," *Seattle Times*, January 31, 2007.

Pamuk, Orhan. "Freedom to Write," *New York Review of Books*, May 25, 2006.

Peters, Robert. "Internet's New 'XXX' District Won't Protect Kids and May Exacerbate Other Pornography Related Problems," Morality in Media, March 6, 2007.

Pilger, John. "The Real First Casualty of War," *New Statesman*, April 24, 2006.

Poniewozik, James. "Blame It on Bauer," *Time*, March 26, 2007.

Quirk, Matthew. "The Web Police: Internet Censorship Is Prevalent Not Just in China but Throughout the World. Can the Web Be Tamed?" *Atlantic*, May 2006.

*Register-Guard.* (Eugene, OR), "Censoring the Internet," July 2, 2008.

Rodgers, Tom. "Children Are Only a Few Clicks Away from Being Exposed to Pornography on MySpace.com," Morality in Media, September 22, 2006.

Rothschild, Matthew. "Mainstream Media Culpability," *Progressive*, July 2008.

Sambrook, Richard. "Regulation, Responsibility, and the Case Against Censorship," *Index on Censorship*, January 2006.

Sardar, Ziauddin. "Freedom of Speech Is Islamic, Too," *New Statesman*, February 13, 2006.

Scales, Pat. "The Good War: If We Don't Fight the Perils of Censorship, We Can't Win," *School Library Journal*, July 2008.

Schwartz, Stephen. "A Miscarriage of Censorship: Federal Prison Officials Need a New Policy for Tackling Extremism," *Weekly Standard*, September 17, 2007.

Taylor, Stuart, Jr. "Free Speech and Double Standards," *National Journal*, September 29, 2007.

Thomas, Mark. "When It Comes to Freedom of Speech We Are Prepared to Defend Only Those Threatened Ideas That We Agree With," *New Statesman*, December 19, 2005.

*USA Today.* "Amendment Supporters Exaggerate Threat to Flag," June 14, 2005.

*Wall Street Journal.* "Fit and Unfit to Print," June 30, 2006.

*Washington Times.* "'Fairness' Is Censorship," June 17, 2008.

Wilson, Chris Smith. "To Read or Not to Read," *Owl*, November 2006.

Wolf, Daniel. "Censorship Wasn't All Bad: Restraints on Speech Have Been Abolished, Says Daniel Wolf, but We Live in a New Age of Social Control," *Spectator*, February 4, 2006.

Younge, Gary. "The Right to Be Offended," *Nation*, February 27, 2006.

# Index

## A

*Abrams v. U.S.* (1919), 19–20
Adult-entertainment industry, 94–96
Adult obscenity, 101, 103–104
Advertising, 89
Alito, Samuel, 13
American Civil Liberties Union (ACLU), 17–24, 79
*American Civil Liberties Union, Reno v.* (1997), 9, 108
American flag
   destruction of, 25–37
   as private property, 34–35
   symbolism of, 35, 37
American Library Association (ALA), 72, 113–115
*American Library Association, United States v.* (2003), 9, 114
Amster, Sara-Ellen, 76–81
Anti-flag-destruction amendment, 26–29, 36
Anti-Semitism, 39
Anti-war leaflets, 19–20
Aristophanes, 75
Artistic works, censorship of, 23–24

## B

Banned Books Week, 72–73
Beeson, Ann, 109
Bipartisan Campaign Reform Act, 15
Black, Hugo, 110
Books
   danger of banning, in schools, 71–75
   parental voice over, in schools, 66–70
Brandeis, Louis D., *19*, 20

Brandenberg standard, 20
*Brandenberg v. Ohio* (1969), 20
*Brokeback Mountain* (Proulx), 73, 75
Bush, George W., 115

## C

Cable television, 62–63, 97–98
California, 79
*California, Miller v.* (1973), 7, 24, 101–102, 106
Campaign-finance laws, 15
*Carnal Knowledge* (film), 107
Cartoons, political, 44–51
Cellular Telecommunications & Internet Association, 95
Censorship
   of artistic works, 23–24
   book, 71–75
   definition of, 7
   governmental, 61–62, 64–65
   of hate speech, 38–43
   of Internet, 89–91, 99–104
   of pornography, 7–8, 10
   teen view of, 84
*Chaplinsky v. New Hampshire* (1942), 22–23, 41
Child Online Protection Act (COPA), 9, 102–103, 108–109
Child pornography, 7, 8, 89–90
Children
   decency standards are needed to protect, 53–59
   parents should monitor television viewing of, 60–65
   protection of, from pornography, 8–10, 94–96, 102–103, 108–109

Children's Internet Protection Act
   (CIPA), 9, 113, 114, 119–121
Children's literature, sex in, 67–68
Children's Television Act, 97
China, 90–91
Cho, Christina, 118–122
Citizens Flag Alliance (CFA), 31–37
Clear and present danger test, 20
Clinton, Bill, 47, 64, 120–121
Clothing bans, 84–85
Communications Decency Act
   (CDA), 9
Community standards, 106–111
Confederate flag, 29
Constitutional rights, of students, 77
Cory, Peter, 39, 43
Coursey, David, 88–92
Cunningham, Randy, 26

D
Danish cartoon controversy, 39–51
Debs, Eugene V., 18
Decency standards
   are necessary, 53–59
   are not necessary, 60–65
Democracy, 78–79, 83
Denmark, 40
Des Moines, Tinker v. (1969), 14, 15,
   20–21, 77
Douglas, William O., 107, 110

E
Economist, 60–65
Edgerton High School, 82–86
Eichman, U.S. v. (1990), 21, 26, 33
Electronic media
   education on use of, 93–98
   regulation of, 88–92
Espionage Act, 18, 20

F
Family Hour, 54–59

Federal Communications
   Commission (FCC), 61, 62, 65,
   96–98
Federal Election Commission v.
   Wisconsin Right to Life, Inc. (2007),
   16
Feldman, Ariel, 118–122
Fighting words, 22–23
Filtering software
   in libraries, 112–117
   problems with, 119–122
First Amendment
   flag burning and, 32–33
   free speech protections and, 7, 9,
      13, 18, 20–24
   obscene materials and, 101–102
   pornography and, 10
   public's views on, 23
   Supreme Court and, 19–20
Fjelstad, Norm, 84–85, 86
Flag desecration
   rulings on, 21, 26, 32, 33
   should be protected, 25–30
   should not be protected, 31–37
Flag Protection Act, 33
Foul language, on television, 55
Frankfurter, Felix, 37
Franklin, Ben, 48
Frederick, Morse v. (2007), 13, 16
Free Expression Policy Project
   (FEPP), 120, 121
Free speech
   limits on, 12–17, 22–24, 82–86
   protection of, 17–24
   public's views on, 40
   for students, 13–15, 76–86
   in U.S., 89–90

G
Gandhi, 50
Georgia, Stanley v. (1969), 7
Goldberg, Jonah, 12–17

H
Hate speech
   censorship of, 38–43
   protection of, 21–22, 29
   public's views on, 40
Havel, Václav, 49, 50
*Hazelwood v. Kuhlmeier* (1988), 79, 83
Heins, Marjorie, 105–111, 118–122
Holmes, Oliver Wendell, *19*, 20
Hughes, Karen, 47

I
Indecency regulations, 61–65, 96–98
Insane Clown Posse, 83–96
Internet
   censorship of, 89–91
   community standards and, 107–111
   library filters on, are necessary, 112–117
   library filters on, threaten freedom, 118–122
Internet pornography
   age restrictions and, 8–10
   censorship of, 99–104
   debate over, 7
   regulation of, 89–90
Islamofacism, 45

J
*Janesville Gazette*, 82–86
Jefferson, Thomas, 33
Johnson, Gregory, 32
Johnson, Lyndon B., 72
*Johnson, Texas v.* (1989), 21, 26, 32, 33
Joyce, James, 24
*Jyllands-Posten* (newspaper), 39, 40–42, 45, 48

K
Keegstra, Jim, 39

Kennedy, Anthony, 13
King, Martin Luther, Jr., 50, 51
Ku Klux Klan, *11*
Kuehne, Mike, 85
*Kuhlmeier, Hazelwood v.* (1988), 79, 83
Kutty, Faisal, 38–43

L
Laws
   in California, 79
   equality under the, 47
   against hate speech, 39–41
   obscenity, 99–111
Libelous statements, 23
Libraries
   CIPA and, 9, 113, 114, 119–121
   complaints filed with, 69
   obscene materials in, 115–116
   policies of, 113–115
   school, 67
Library Internet filters
   are necessary, 112–117
   threaten freedom, 118–122
Lien, Lawrence, *62*
Loyalty oaths, 20
*Lysistrata* (Aristiphanes), 75

M
Madison, James, 33
Malicious statements, 23
Mapplethorpe, Robert, 24
Marlette, Doug, 44–51
Martin, Kevin J., 97
McCain-Feingold law, 15
McCarthyism, 20
McMasters, Paul K., 93–98
Medals of Honor, 37
Media industry, 64
Meredith, James, 18
Merrion, Jeff, 83, 85
Miller test, 7–8, 24, 106–107
*Miller v. California* (1973), 7, 24, 101–102, 106–107

Minors. *See* Children

Mohammed, depicted in cartoons, 38–51

*Morse v. Frederick* (2007), 13, 16

**N**

National security, 22

Nazi swastika, 29

*New Hampshire, Chaplinsky v.* (1942), 22–23, 41

*New York Times, U.S. v.* (1971), 22

*New York Times Co. v. Sullivan* (1964), 23

Nichols, Mike, 107

**O**

Obscene material, 7–8, 23–24, 101–102, 115–116
*See also* Pornography

Obscenity laws
Internet pornography and, 99–104
should be eliminated, 105–111
support for enforcement of, 103, 104

Offensive speech, self-censorship of, 44–51

*Ohio, Brandenberg v.* (1969), 20

**P**

Palaima, Thomas G., 71–75

Parents
on books in schools, 66–70
online monitoring by, 95
should monitor children's television, 60–65

Parents Television Council (PTC), 53–59

*Paris Adult Theater I v. Slaton* (1973), 102

Pentagon Papers, 22

Permits, 21

Peters, Robert, 99–104

Political cartoons, 44–51

Political protests, 21, 77–78

Political speech, 13, 14, 15

Pornography
age restrictions on, 8–10
censorship of, 7–8, 10
child, 7, 8, 89–90
court rulings on, 7
on electronic devices, 94–96
hardcore, 101
libraries and, 115–116
three-pronged test for, 7–8, 24, 106
*See also* Internet pornography

Private property, flag and, 34–35

Protests, 21, 77–78

Proulx, Annie, 73, 75

Public libraries. *See* Libraries

Public officials, libelous statements about, 23

**R**

*Reno v. American Civil Liberties Union* (1997), 9, 108

Reruns, 57

Responsibility, 49–50

Richardson, Cindy, 86

Richardson, Matthew D., 84, 85

Roberts, John G., 13

Rushdie, Salman, 47

**S**

Sargent, John, 69

Satellite television, 62–63, 97–98

Sawicki, Arlene, 112–117

Scalia, Antonin, 13

*Schenck v. U.S.* (1919), 19

Schools
book banning in, 71–75
clothing bans in, 84–85
free speech in, 13–15, 76–86
parents should have say about books in, 66–70

Self-censorship, 44–51

Set-top boxes, 63–64

Sexual content
in children's literature, 67–70
electronic devices and, 94–96
on television, 55–56

Shamlian, Janet, 67, 69

*Slaton, Paris Adult Theater I v.* (1973), 102

*Stanley v. Georgia* (1969), 7

Stern, Howard, 89

Stevens, John Paul, 7

Stewart, Potter, 24

Street, Sidney, 18

Student protests, 77–78

Student speech
limits on, 13–15, 82–86
should be free, 76–81
views on, 80

*Sullivan, New York Times Co. v.* (1964), 23

Supreme Court, First Amendment and, 19–20

Sweden, 89

Symbolic speech, 20–21

Symbolism, of flag, 35, 37


T

Taylor, Laurie, 67–69

Technology
education on use of, 93–98
regulation of new, 88–92
television filtering, 63–64

Teen sexuality, 67–68

Television
cable and satellite, 62–63, 97–98
decency standards for, 53–59
parents should regulate, 60–65

Television advertising, 89

*Texas v. Johnson* (1989), 21, 26, 32, 33

Thomas, Carleen, 106, 108

Thomas, Clarence, 13, 109

Thomas, Robert, 106, 108

Threats, 21–22

Throckmorton, Warren, 66–70

*Tinker v. Des Moines* (1969), 14, *15*, 20–21, 77

Trudeau, Garry, 46


U

*Ulysses* (Joyce), 24

*United States v. American Library Association* (2003), 9, 114

*United States v. Eichman* (1990), 21, 26, 33

*U.S., Abrams v.* (1919), 19–20

*U.S., Schenck v.* (1919), 19

*U.S. v. New York Times* (1971), 22


V

Van Gogh, Theo, 47

V-chips, 63–64

Viacom Inc., 97

Viewpoint discrimination, 21

Violence, on television, 56

Volokh, Eugene, 29


W

Warner, James H., 29

White, Byron, 35

Winter, Tim, *58*

*Wisconsin Right to Life, Inc., Federal Election Commission v.* (2007), 16


Y

Young, Cathy, 25–30

# Picture Credits

AP Images, 34, 42, 58, 62, 68, 74, 78, 85, 90, 97, 101, 109, 116, 121

© Bettmann/Corbis, 19

Jim Bourg/Reuters/Landov, 28

Robert Galbraith/Reuters/Landov, 87

© Dennis MacDonald/Alamy, 15

© Jenny Matthews/Alamy, 8

David Maxwell/AFP/Getty Images, 11

© Keith Morris/Alamy, 52

MPI/Hulton Archive/Getty Images, 46

Steve Zmina, 14, 23, 27, 36, 40, 56, 63, 73, 80, 84, 95, 103, 114